Jack Arrington was a man of acti  game nor have good intentions, was with a boldness and confide decided from an early age he wo worry what others thought of him, no, he would study/ research, and then move. Hold on!

He has written an authentic story of his life and how he overcame many challenges. His difficult circumstances didn't define him but made him stronger and more resilient. He was a serial entrepreneur, and yet he also kept life's priorities in line. His faith and family were preeminent.

And his constant love for his wife Kathy and their courtship make this a romance story too.

Jack's story is the American dream, and his simple wisdoms and homespun style can benefit anyone that wants to become the best version of themselves.

Dave Zillig
DAZSER Companies Founder

If you think you cannot be a success. If you think you cannot overcome the things that are holding you back. Stop now and read this book. It is filled with real-world truth that will help you reshape your thinking – change what you believe is possible – and give you the courage to step into your dreams and make them happen. Jack's honest – funny – brilliant insight in *Without a Dime* is a must read!

Pam Wolf
Author, Speaker, Business Success Coach

Jack Arrington merges practical ideas and strategies with hilarious real life experiences to reveal simple but brilliant pearls of wisdom. *Without a Dime* is an easy read for anyone looking to think better in business and in life.

Bill Covington
Stormfitters Corp. President, CEO

Jack was committed to his faith and has lived it for the 40 years that I knew him. His story will encourage anyone regardless of their background or education. The proven business principles in his book will inspire you to look not just at circumstances and unfortunate occurrences in your life but rather to hard work, discipline, and commitment. His book illustrates that by practice in biblical principles, success is available to all.

Tom Chapman
Founder and former owner of Advanced Protection Technologies, Managing Member of CG Land Services, LLC, Entrepreneur, Author of *Make All You Can, Give All You Can*

Jack Arrington was one of the most loving, giving, pure hearted and wise men I have ever met.

His life was an inspiration to me as it reflected the integrity, character and light of Christ in everything he did and said.

I was privileged to have been the recipient of his kind and generous spirit for years, when he faithfully served as a volunteer, advisor, and contributor during fundraising events at the ministries of New Life Solutions. His counsel to me as the Director of Special Events has made a huge impact on the success of these events. He encouraged and reminded me in times of stress that " *God is not nervous!*" I have written these words on my office whiteboard, where I see them every day as a reminder and have shared them with several visitors who are facing difficult situations. Unfortunately, Jack is absent from our lives here on earth, but his mentorship and words of wisdom continue to inspire and bless others!

Gail Freedman-Barrett
Special Events Director of New Life Solutions

It's Much More than a Dime

A Bucket Full of Dimes should be the real title of Jack Arrington's book full of how life experiences good and bad lead us to become better business leaders, entrepreneurs and humans . It is a quick, easy read that you won't want to put down until you finish that last page of his everyday experiences turned into business axioms and advice for a well lived life. Sometimes you will laugh, sometimes you will cry and most times you will nod in agreement that his advice is worth taking to heart and applying in your own business, large or small, and personal journey through life.

As a long time small business owner and friend of Jack, I so very much appreciate that he has left us with his unique style of encouragement and examples to follow that can enrich our lives. This is truly the essence of Jack Arrington. It is his deeds, his thoughts on life magnified in writing and of this one man's ups, downs, business success, and overall warmth and love of family that should be on everyone's must read "bucket" list.

Cheryl Harris
President of CRG, Inc. , Association Management and Event Planning

You would have been blessed to have known Jack Arrington. He was a natural leader and friend to all that came across his path. His book shares proven principles and examples of how to have a successful life in business, marriage, and having a purposeful influence on others. You will learn and also be blessed beyond measure when reading *Without a Dime*.

Joseph Pippen
Attorney, Author, and host of radio show *ASK AN ATTORNEY*

Without a Dime

27 Powerful Secrets

Life, Love & Business

Jack Arrington

ISBN-13: 978-1-945975-94-3
ISBN-10: 1945975946

Published by EA Books Publishing a division of
Living Parables of Central Florida, Inc. a 501c3
EABooksPublishing.com

"If you are not drawing your own lines,
you are coloring in someone else's dream."

– *Jack Arrington*

DEDICATION

I would like to thank my beautiful wife Kathy for sharing her love, joy, encouragement, and enthusiasm as I was writing this book. Her unwavering faith in me made what seemed impossible become a reality.

ACKNOWLEDGEMENTS

From a grateful heart, many thanks to our dear friend, Kay Daly, for the numerous sacrificial hours, days and months that you invested in helping me become an author. Together we took some very rough drafts off numerous yellow legal pads and transformed the words into book form. You were very patient, talented and you did a great job!

To Kathy, Tim, Christy, Casey, Corey and Cydney: You are forever woven into the fabric of my life. I love you!

Profound thanks go to Natalie Gillespie. Natalie, you are an exceptionally talented editor who took the manuscript of this book and made the true life story become a legacy gift. Your organizational skills are second to none. Your keen insights captured every heartbeat of the stories and principles that are keyed to the original message while honoring Jack's unique writing style and his special twist on storytelling. Well done!

To the talented team of EA Books Publishing: Cheri, Kristen, Jessie, Michelle, and Bob, your skills took a manuscript and enabled it to blast off of the launching pad! Each of you made significant contributions to the publishing process that took this work across the finish line. It was a joy to partner with each of you!

Craig Gaines, you did a great job capturing the original book cover design that Jack envisioned. Thank you!

To the many family members, friends and fellow entrepreneurs who encouraged along the way and shared thoughts when shown glimpses of this book, your wise counsel was received with love and in many cases caused changes to be made in this book. Thank you!

TABLE OF CONTENTS

Dedication   i

Acknowledgements   ii

Table of Contents   iii

Foreword by Kathy Arrington   v

Introduction   vii

Fiery Explosions of Common Sense   1

Without A Dime   10

Bad Boys Can Become Heroes   15

Plugging the Piehole   27

Right Into My Lap and Upside Down   36

I Hope You Learn to Dance   46

Gently Kissed Her Tears Away   58

Miss Universe: More Than A Beauty Queen   68

Secret Entrance to the Exit   75

Ph.D.: Past Having Doubts   83

Oh Happy Day! God Is Not Nervous   94

She Is Not Yours. She Is Mine   100

Escape Into the Light   105

The Ice Box Ate Me   112

Darth Vader Was Driving   116

Well, You Do the Math!   123

Smooth-Talking Stranger in a Silk Suit   132

Laughing Grass   142

Closing Thoughts   146

Afterword   147

Photographs   160

Success Secrets Legend   169

Recommended Resources   173

The Arrington Legacy:
Businesses Owned By Jack Arrington   174

Endnotes   175

FOREWORD

Dear Reader,

Two months after Jack penned the closing paragraph of this book, his profound closing words proved to be prophetic. One week after being diagnosed with pancreatic cancer that had already spread to his liver and lungs, my darling husband quickly and peacefully left our home and entered through the Gates of Glory to his eternal home. After twenty-seven years of separation on earth, he was reunited with our son Kenny. I know that the Father greeted him with those wonderful words, "Well done, good and faithful servant! You have been faithful with a few things; I will put you in charge of many things. Come and share your master's happiness!" (Matthew 25:23, NIV)

Jack's wish in his final days and my last promise to him was to see that his book was published. You are holding in your hands a work that was almost impossible to accomplish. Jack was a man who could not spell, yet he labored intensely to write this so beautifully. My very successful man was unstoppable once he set a goal! His desire was to mentor and coach businessmen and women to be the very best they could be in every area of their lives. I pray this book accomplishes that worthy goal in your life.

Several months after his passing, I searched through Jack's daily calendar to see what his last entries may have been. He was forever working on being the best man he could be and was known to write some of his motivational goals at the top of his daily calendar to remind himself to stay on target. His habit was to write these goals or inspirations repeatedly ahead in the calendar on days yet to come. At the top of the page for July 8, 2015, the day he took his last breath, he had written:

Do I Live? Do I Love? Do I Matter?

Yes, my darling, you did live, you certainly did love, and you very much mattered.

As you read Jack's words of wisdom, dear readers, I pray they will inspire you toward your own success, and that you will live each moment to the fullest.

Kathy Arrington, Jack's Childhood Sweetheart and Devoted Wife of Fifty-One Beautiful Years

INTRODUCTION

Early one cool morning at Yosemite, just as the sun was coming up and the mist from the river was rising, I sat down at the picnic table on our deck with my plate of bacon and a steaming cup of coffee. Instantly, a three-foot-tall, black-and-white eagle swooped down into my plate. Her sharp talons grabbed all four slices of crisp bacon as she pierced me with her bright yellow irises surrounded by pitch-black pupils. Her enormous hooked beak hovered a mere six inches from my face. She looked me straight in the eyes. Terrifying! In a split second, she stole all of my bacon and took off, quickly vanishing from my sight.

If you are fed up with your hard-earned bacon being stolen from you – leaving you terrified, broke, and unable to enjoy your life to the fullest, I have good news. I wrote this book you hold in your hands just for you.

I mean it.

Just. For. You.

See, I started my adult life without a dime. I had no education. Even into my thirties I could not read or write. Spelling never did become my forte. However, I became a self-made millionaire (and I married Miss Universe, but that's a story for later in the book).

Today is your day.

The time is *now*.

You can do it too. I know you can, because I did. I started without a dime to my name. I could not read. I could not write. But I knew I could do something big. You can too. These pages hold secret keys to unlock powerful ways to change your thinking and answer the questions: *Do I live? Do I love? Do I matter?*

This book imparts secrets to help focus your thoughts and actions to become more productive and on-track for success. I sandwich these success secrets between real-life stories from my own experiences that are heartwarming and often humorous. I also include practical tips for business success I call "Pure Veins of Gold." Put these tips into practice and you will strike the mother lode. I guarantee you'll be inspired to become your best self when you apply my solid, sound life and business principles to help you take home the gold in life, love and business.

Let me let you in on one secret right off the bat: Good news. No matter what your circumstances look like now, keep reading. In the end, you win!

Fiery Explosions of Common Sense

Success Secret No. 1: Truth means agreement with reality, even if others don't get it.

Success Secret No. 2: You first must have an understanding to have a revelation.

I was sixty days into my sophomore year of high school when I heard my name over the loudspeaker system, a sound I heard often during my school years. "Jack Arrington, come to the principal's office immediately."

I knew from experience this was not good. When I arrived at the office, a red-faced Mr. Goldberg barked, "Sit down and shut up!" I had not even spoken. The man looked like he was on fire. Imagine Albert Einstein in full ruddy-faced rage, fist pounding the desk as he hollered, and you'll get the idea.

"All your teachers are upset with you and me because you won't follow their instructions," Goldberg shouted. "You think you are smarter than all of us, Jack. But you are sixteen years old, you can't even read, and you sure can't spell. How in the world did you get to high school anyhow?

"Jack, you are so stupid you would not even know if your pants were on fire. You must leave this school now and never come back. Do. You. Understand?" The man looked apoplectic as his fist continued to pound, punctuating each word of his grim pronouncement.

When the principal seemed to stop for breath, I asked, "Can I talk now?"

Goldberg nodded reluctantly.

"Is this about math class yesterday?" I said. " Well, the teacher was wrong and I told her so."

"What did you tell her, Jack?" Goldberg wanted to know. "Tell me the truth."

"Well, she was telling everyone in the class, 'If Bob swims ten laps in the pool and it takes him one minute per lap, and the pool is one hundred feet long, how long will it take him to swim the ten laps?' She told everyone the answer is ten minutes. But that's not true. Bob is going to get tired and will not be able to maintain a one-minute lap. He will never make it in ten minutes," I said.

While my teacher was trying to teach black-and-white computation, I could see this was not the whole picture. Sadly, my teacher did not appreciate my reasoning. Logic and math did not go hand-in-hand that day. However, I learned a truth I call Secret No. 1.

Success Secret No. 1:

Truth means agreement with reality, even if others don't get it.

What do I mean by this? I mean truth is not always as it appears to be. You need to add in common sense. On paper, in black-and-white in my math book, that boy could swim ten laps in ten minutes. In real life, the truth is that muscle fatigue would need to be taken into consideration when factoring the amount of laps that boy could swim in the time given. In fact, truth taken to an extreme can become a lie. Truth goes deeper; consequences and results are factors in determining truth. When you are looking for the truth in a situation or circumstance, make sure it agrees with reality. This is the first Success Secret.

Just before I was thrown out of school, I was told by some teachers that I needed to go to trade school to learn how to weld or be a mechanic. Over the years I was told by teachers and administrators that I was a "dummy" and stupid. It was so embarrassing never being chosen to participate in a spelling bee or asked to read aloud. I grew petrified with fear if I heard my name called out in class.

The day I was thrown out of high school, I felt distraught. I cried bitterly, muttering to myself, *At least I'm not ugly, a dummy, and stupid.* I rode my motor scooter home, still crying and feeling bad about myself. In that moment, I promised myself I would show them all they were wrong. I was hurt and depressed. But I decided I had to get a job and snap out of this blue attitude right then. I decided their "truth" about me was not in agreement with my reality, the reality that I was going to make something of myself and show them all how wrong they were about me.

My first job entailed cleaning a barbershop. After five o'clock, six days a week, I cleaned up at the barbershop. It took me one hour and the owner gave me fifty cents a day. He also gave me valuable lessons about cash flow, explaining cash flow to me as he stacked the money he made that day on the counter. The barber had a safe in the back of the shop that was full of money. I asked him what he was going to do with his money. "I am going to buy this building, this shop and the two shops next door, to rent out. That will give me more cash flow."

I'm going to need more cash flow when I tell my mom and dad I was permanently thrown out of school, I lamented to myself.

When my dad got home from work, I told him what happened. He looked at me for a long time and then asked me what I had done to get thrown out of school. I told him the math story of the boy in the pool. He took his time thinking, and then he nodded and said I was one hundred percent right. Boy, did that make me feel better.

***

My father never went to school. He grew up on a farm in Kentucky. The cows and the livestock were more important than a book-learned education. But he had incredible common sense, including all he learned from his father and grandfather. My father was only ten years old when his father put him in charge of the moonshine still. His dad, my grandfather, told my dad never to let the temperature gauge go past the red line on the cooker, but my grandpa did not tell his son what could happen if it did. Well, Dad did put too much wood under the cooker and went outside the small shed to work. He was about twenty-five feet away when *kaboom*! A fiery explosion lit the sky. Dad showed me the nail scars in his leg and said those scars were a reminder of the past. He then taught me a truth about understanding and revelation. This is accurate thinking, and I call it Success Secret No. 2.

Success Secret No. 2:

You first must have an understanding to have a revelation.

My dad heard my grandfather say not to let the moonshine still get too hot. He didn't mean to drift away and forget to keep a close eye on it. But he had no firsthand knowledge or experience of what would happen if the temperature gauge went into the red. When that still blew up and left him with nails embedded in his legs, understanding became revelation. The revelation was this: You must pay close attention and tend to the job at hand. For my dad, it was a fiery explosion of common sense. For you and me, it means applying common sense before you have to learn a tough lesson the hard way – like your moonshine still blowing up.

***

Early morning the day after I got kicked out of school, I was out the door looking for a fulltime job. I was sixteen and strong. I had a lot of common sense. And that was the extent of my resume. That and the cleaning job at the barbershop.

I could not fill out an application for employment because I couldn't read or write. I had passed kindergarten through eighth grade without ever becoming literate. I didn't pass so much as pass through each grade. Words were a jumble of letters to me. When I tried to write, the letters were scrambled and no one else could read them. I know now I have a learning disability that back then went undiagnosed. There were no dyslexics in the 1950s, only "dummies." Still, I had common sense, self-motivation, and persistence, traits that would be invaluable for me in the coming years.

 I rode up and down neighborhood streets on my motor scooter, looking for work. Then I saw a man from a local lawn service mowing a yard. I pulled over and approached him. With the mower still running, he stopped.

"I want to work for you!" I hollered.

"What did you say again?" The man yelled back.

"I want to work for you," I repeated.

To my amazement, the stranger turned off the mower and said, "Okay."

Training started immediately.

"Don't put your hands or feet under the mower," he said. "Run as fast as you can and don't miss anything."

Just like that, I had a job. The owner got three dollars and fifty cents per lawn and four dollars for a corner lot. He paid me thirty-five cents a lawn. I worked about sixty hours a week and made thirty dollars. This was big money to me. *Cash flow.* The lawn man demanded cash on the spot from his customers as soon as we were done. If the homeowner was not there, they arranged to leave the payment under the doormat before we cut the grass. If the money was not there, we would not mow.

The lawn man was in charge of cash flow. He also received tips. He told me about Christmas tips. He would average one hundred dollars in tips, all pure profit. He was extremely disciplined and only did one thing fast and well: cut grass at a very cheap price on the day he said he would be there. All the lawns we serviced were quite close together. Neighbors would walk up to him and ask him the cost for mowing their lawn. When he told them the price, they usually said yes. He then nicely told people who were far outside his driving pattern that he could no longer service them. Profits kept going up.

I got up early and was on the job by six o'clock every morning. I had to bring my lunch and work fast to keep up with this man. He had a truck, four push mowers, four brooms, three file sharpeners, and two gas cans. As he drove to the job location, I would turn the mowers on their sides and sharpen the blades with the file. Then I would top off the gas. We never wasted time. Never.

Production and efficiency were all that mattered. I look back on those times, and I am amazed that between the gas fumes and filing metal blades we didn't blow ourselves up. If a mower broke, we grabbed another and kept going. At the end of the day, we had to gas up the truck and repair anything broken so that everything was ready for the next day.

When I first went to work, I passed out from the heat. My boss was furious with me for holding up production. "That will never happen again," he said. From that day forward, he made me drink a quart of water before I started so that I was completely hydrated. Working in intense heat and humidity, if the body starts out dehydrated, it can never catch up.

Although the lawn man may not have had a college degree, he had plenty of common sense he applied to his business. I watched and learned from the lawn service owner. Some of the things I learned were pure veins of gold. I worked hard, not only mowing lawns, but also learning to mine for these gold nuggets that made his business a success.

Years later, I saw an episode of the animated TV series *SpongeBob SquarePants*, where the character Mr. Crabby opened his store twenty-four hours every day. SpongeBob was thrilled to have the opportunity to work day and night. I felt like SpongeBob, really happy to work all the time.

I learned that good service at a good price equaled cash in the lawn man's pocket on a regular basis. By paying an employee (me) a small portion, he increased his cash flow with additional income from the lawns I mowed. Truth was now lining up with my reality. I was not a dummy. I could succeed through drive and determination. Plus, I was quickly gathering business revelation because of my new understanding of how cash flow works.

Strike it Rich!

Success Secret No. 1: Truth means agreement with reality, even if others don't get it.

Success Secret No. 2: You first must have understanding to have revelation.

Pure Veins of Gold

These are the "gold nuggets," practical business tips I mined from my lawn maintenance job. They still hold true for any service business today.

1. If you are in the service business, apply the words spoken by one of my first bosses: "Run as fast as you can and don't miss anything." Work quickly but do the job thoroughly. When you work fast, you have time to take on more customers. However, you must do a thorough job without missing anything or you'll lose the customers you have.

2. Expect payment on the spot. Even better, ask the customer to pay upfront. That way, you'll never have to do the extra work of collections, and you will never work for free.

3. Consider hiring someone under you and paying that worker a portion of what the whole job pays. That way, you start running a business rather than doing all the manual work yourself. You start making "active" income (the money you did the work for) and "passive" income (money from the work your employees did that you keep a portion of before paying them).

4. Price your service right. My lawn boss offered to cut grass for a cheaper price than the competition. He got a lot of customers because the price was right.

5. Keep your customers geographically close together. The less time you have to spend traveling to reach your customers, the more time you have to do the work and take on new customers. Politely turn down customers who are outside of your geographic limits. Politeness is key. You may need them again in the future.

Without a Dime

Success Secret No. 3: Setting goals is one of the most important things you do to succeed in life and business.

I grew up with my two cousins, Hager and Gary Arrington. Hager was the older. He and I were the same age, twelve years old at the time of the story I'm about to share. Gary had just turned seven. Hager had a Vespa motor scooter and he took me for a ride. I never knew anyone could fall in love with a piece of sheet metal with tires, but I did. I have got to have one, I said to myself.

When Hager, Gary, and I went to the amusement park one Saturday, we rode the bus. It was a great day of fun and laughter. We spent all our money except for fifty cents for the bus ride home. Twenty-five cents for me. Twenty-five cents for Hagar. Maybe we could slide Gary in under the radar. We jumped on the bus, put our fifty cents in, and went to sit down.

"Wait a minute," the bus driver said. "How old is he?" He pointed at Gary.

"Six," Hagar and I said in unison.

"Seven!" Gary hollered. "I am seven. I had a birthday!"

"No, he is six," I said nervously, giving Gary the stink eye. Kids seven to eleven paid a ten-cent fare. Six and under were free.

The bus was packed with people. Everyone was laughing. Now Gary started chanting, "Seven! Seven! Seven!" The driver said I needed ten more cents for him.

"I'm without a dime," I said.

After the bus driver had his fun at our expense, he told the three of us to sit down. People on the bus were still laughing as I sat there embarrassed and scared. Gary was still chanting, "Seven! Seven! Seven!" I told myself I would never lie again. I also promised myself I would never again be without a dime. I can still hear, "Seven! Seven! Seven!" in my head at times. Without even realizing it, I was beginning to set goals for myself.

Goal No. 1: No lying.

Goal No. 2: Have money at all times!

My desire for a motor scooter like the one Hager had just kept growing. I decided I had to have a Cushman Eagle motor scooter. It cost three hundred and twenty-five dollars, an incredibly large amount of money. I had three dollars and twenty-five cents. All I needed was ninety-nine percent more. I told my dad what I was doing and he gave his permission, but I don't think he really thought I could accomplish it when he said, "Okay."

Success Secret No. 3:

Setting goals is one of the most important things you do to succeed in life and business.

My sister sent away for a poster of a teal Cushman Eagle motor scooter. I put it on the wall in my bedroom and looked at it a million times. I could feel the wind in my face. I was twelve years old and I still had to go to school. How in the world was I going to get the money?

At that time, we lived in a subdivision of one-story homes in St. Petersburg, Fla., called Orange Hill. The houses were built in an old orange grove. I went around the neighborhood and asked our neighbors if I could pick their oranges. Then I sold them. My dad frequently said to me, "Ask and you will receive."

One day, I saw a man down the street cutting down old dead orange trees. I saw him almost every day, because many trees in the neighborhood were dying. I decided to walk over and ask if I could help. As I got closer, he was screaming the F-word at his chainsaw.

"What the hell do you want?" He said.

"I need money," I said.

"Get out of here," he said.

About a week later, he was removing trees at the house next door to mine. There were piles of limbs everywhere.

"You still need money, Boy?" He said when he spotted me.

"Yes, Sir," I said.

He told me my job was to sharpen the ax as sharp as a razor and to pick up limbs and throw them in the truck.

"I'll pay you to help me," he said.

That summer I learned how to work hard. No matter what kind of weather, starting at the crack of dawn we worked. In south Florida, tropical storms are common. This particular summer was no exception. We worked through rain, lightning, and extreme heat. Incidentally, this was the summer I also learned every vulgar curse word in the book, courtesy of my new boss. I began to use them as "sentence enhancers." I shocked all my friends (and adults) with my newfound vocabulary. Later in life I learned this was not an admirable or appreciated asset. (In fact, curse words in many circles can be a liability.)

Each day, I got three dollars to add to my scooter fund. It took me two years to get all the cash together, but I finally did it. My new motor scooter was the most important thing in my life. I did not realize at the time what all this determination did for me. I became more confident and much wiser. I would go on to set many more goals for my life. The self-discipline it took for an adolescent to save his money instead of spend it was enormous. And enormously satisfying in the end, as I proudly rode my new scooter. As the saying goes, I now knew I could "Git r done," and I had more common sense than ever.

Strike it Rich!

Success Secret No. 3: Setting goals is one of the most important things you do to succeed in life and business.

Pure Veins of Gold

1. Be willing to start at the bottom of the totem pole. No job is too small. No work is too menial if you see it as a learning opportunity and stepping-stone to your next goal.

2. Learn to save your money. No matter how little you make, "pay yourself" by saving some. This money can then accumulate and be available for bigger purchases later on.

3. Learn to wait for what you want. Self-discipline and self-control may not be fun exercises when the paycheck is hot in your hands, but they are invaluable character traits. As a kid, an impatient young boy, I waited two years to save enough for that Vespa. Two years to an adolescent might as well have been forever! But the payoff in the end made the wait worth it. Start saving now. Today! You will never regret it. The self-discipline you develop will pay off in many areas of your life.

4. Dream bigger than you think you can achieve. Dream bigger than those around you think you can achieve. Then set out to prove everyone wrong. I love this quote from *Paradigms* author and businessman Joel A. Barker, who said: "Vision without action is merely a dream. Action without vision just passes the time. Vision with action can change the world."[1]

Bad Boys Can Become Heroes

Success Secret No. 4: Learning from our experiences, both positive and negative, makes us more efficient and effective. We must be flexible and change our behavior or activities to improve ourselves and our situation.

At fifteen I entered the eighth grade at Lealman Junior High School. I had attended eight different schools by this time because my family moved a lot, and it took me ten years of schooling to finally enter the eighth grade. Being held back and struggling to learn meant I spent plenty of time in meetings with teachers, guidance counselors, and principals. To cover up all my academic shortcomings, I became a smartass. I acted tough. I disrespected and made fun of teachers and authority. Capitalizing on my gift for humor became a big part of my survival method in school. My saving grace was probably my common sense, as well as my ability to continue to set goals for myself to succeed (just not necessarily in school).

My close friend Jerry was about as smart as I was, but poor Jerry had no common sense to save him. He failed to learn from any of his considerable negative experiences.

Success Secret No. 4:

Learning from our experiences, both positive and negative, makes us more efficient and effective. We must be flexible and change our behavior or activities to improve ourselves and our situation

To show our classmates how tough we were, Jerry and I launched a contest to see who could get the most whacks on the rear end from the principal in a week. Mr. Moore used a big wooden paddle, a three-foot-long weapon with holes drilled in it. He would grip it by the handle with his two meaty hands and swing it like a lumberjack swings an ax. The rest of the school could hear every thwack and keep score. My butt was black-and-blue, but I was determined to win. We were the bad boys of the school but thought we were the school's heroes by standing against authority.

One day, Jerry and I were on the outside basketball court when Mr. Moore came out to his car to go to lunch.

"Have a great lunch, Chili," Jerry hollered.

Mr. Moore hated being called that name. Infuriated, he charged towards us. He grabbed us by the necks and dragged us inside. He always administered our paddlings outside his office in the hallway. It was a two-story building and each *thwack* reverberated throughout the school.

Jerry and I knew the drill: Wait in the hall, put our hands on the wall with our legs and feet spread out, about twelve inches away from the wall. Be ready for three to five whacks.

Mr. Moore marched into the hall with his paddle. The fuming principal grabbed Jerry, spun him around and hit him on his bottom as hard as I had ever seen. There was just one problem. Jerry was not ready.

His hands were just going up to brace himself when the paddle came down and Jerry's forehead and face smashed into the concrete wall. He fell to the floor like a five-foot scarecrow with no straw and no life. In terror, I thought, *He's dead, He's dead, and I'm next.* That is all my mind could imagine at the time. Mr. Moore looked down at Jerry in shock. Jerry did not move. He was out cold. Mr. Moore stood there staring, his weapon of choice in his hand. He suddenly turned as white as a sheet as the fear of what he had done started to set in.

I had my hands on the wall ready to die next. Mr. Moore started really sweating. "Keep your mouth shut," he said, glaring into my eyes. "Don't say a word. Now get out of here."

I did not see or hear from Jerry the rest of the day. I felt petrified with fear. All I could think of was Mr. Moore carrying Jerry's body through the woods in the back of the school to bury him. I did not say a word the rest of the day.

As I was about to leave school, Jerry came walking across the lawn, as usual, to ride home with me. He had a big knot on his forehead and a bigger smile on his face.

"What happened?" I asked.

"I woke up in Mr. Moore's arms and he carried me back to his office," he said. "We spent the rest of the afternoon together. He got me milk and cookies and later we had watermelon. Once you get to know him, he's really a nice guy."

On the way home I thought to myself, *I have got to get some new friends.* But it took a while before I listened to my own advice.

***

Jerry and I had more than one person tell us we were going to jail and to hell together. After the face-smashing incident, we were able to stay out of trouble for about thirty days. Then trouble came to us.

It was pitch black outside, about nine o'clock one evening. Jerry and I were sitting on some big rocks down in a twenty-foot ditch, smoking cigars. We could hear a police siren blaring above us. Then a car slowed down above us, and something sailed down from above, hitting and bouncing over the rocks. Police cars went whizzing by.

Afterwards, we began looking for whatever had been tossed. It was too dark to see, but we had two packs of matchbooks. Jerry lit a match. Then we saw it. We thought we had hit the mother lode. We weren't sure what it was, but we were sure we were going to hit it big. Jerry opened a canvas bag and found boxes about eight-by-ten inches each, wrapped in brown paper with string around them.

I was so excited I kept burning my fingers as the matches burned down. Jerry ripped the paper around the boxes.

"Show me the money; show me the money," I said.

We were going to be rich.

Just as Jerry got the cover off the boxes, I was so excited and nervous that I dropped the matches and they went out. It was as dark as the inside of a cow. On our hands and knees, we felt the ground and rocks around us for the book of matches. Finally, we got a match lit and held it close to the open box in Jerry's hands.

"What the heck is this?" I exclaimed. *What were colored pictures of naked women doing in my box of cash?*

We lit another match. We saw picture after picture of men and women with no clothes on. This was back in 1957, and no one had pictures like these *in color!* We opened the second box looking for cash. No cash, just more pictures. We were out of matches now, our hearts pounding with excitement and fear. We could hear a car coming back. The ditch had a big drainage pipe that ran under the road. We knew it very well, even though it was too dark to see. We entered and stumbled our way to the other side. The car stopped on the street above us. We could hear two men talking.

"Can't see a thing. We'll come back at daylight," a man said.

"Let's put the bags back and get out of here," I whispered to Jerry.

"No way!" Jerry said.

Now, I had never heard the word pornography, but over the next few weeks I discovered it. Often. I went home that night to ponder what had just happened. Jerry took our new treasure bag home and hid it in his mother's garage. The next morning we set off for school, talking all the way about the events of the night before. After school we raced home to check and see if we missed something. Maybe there was money in the bags somewhere.

Jerry's mom worked and did not get home until six thirty that night. That gave us three hours. We opened the boxes and looked at the pictures, sifting through the images, telling each other there had to be money somewhere. We were thirteen years old and kept looking and looking. The images caught our attention, and we started saying things like, "I did not know you could do that," and, "Why would you want to?"

There was no money. Jerry kept talking about money.

"I have an idea," he finally said. "Let's hold the pictures for ransom." This was the biggest word I ever heard Jerry use in his life.

"Jerry, we can't hold the pictures for ransom," I said. "We stole them." I could see Jerry's mind working and it was not a pretty sight.

"I got it," Jerry said. "We will sell them at school for twenty-five cents each."

"That's a real bad idea, Jerry," I said.

Jerry started counting the pictures. "I think there are 588 or more," he said. "At twenty-five cents, Jack, how much would that be?"

I was good with numbers. I did not know the alphabet, nor could I read, but I could add. "About one hundred and fifty dollars," I replied.

"I am rich! I'm rich! I'm rich!" Jerry crowed.

"This is really a bad idea," I tried to tell Jerry again, but there was no stopping him. His mind was made up.

About three weeks passed. Then on a Monday morning around eleven o'clock, I was sitting in class when over the loudspeaker I heard, "Jack Arrington, come to the principal's office. Now!" My heart sank. I knew this was not good. As I explained earlier, Principal Moore and I were very close. But not in a good way.

Immediately, all types of bad things began running through my mind. I decided today was the day he was finally going to kill me. I shuffled to the office.

"Don't sit down. They want you inside right now," the receptionist said.

As I walked in, I saw many parents in the room. "That's one of the boys," I heard one say. "That's Jack."

Who are they? I thought. As the door to Mr. Moore's inner sanctum opened, I encountered the St. Petersburg Police Chief standing there in full dress uniform. The principal and vice principal and other teachers were there, as well as – you guessed it – Jerry. Jerry the rat.

The principal grabbed me by the neck and pushed me over the top of his desk. About twenty of the pictures of one of the naked women were displayed there. "Is this your sister?" Moore demanded. For some reason, Jerry told the adults in the room that the girls in the pictures we found were my older sisters. Jerry had thrown me under the bus.

I had no choice but to lie. I was nearly crying by now. "It kind of looks like her," I said, squinting.

"What do you mean, it kind of looks likes her?" Moore said.

"I-I-I'm not sure," I stammered. "I've never seen my sister without her clothes on."

I could not help myself. You have to admit, that was a good one. My impertinent, cheeky sense of humor and attitude were out of control. But this was no time to be a smartass. Mr. Moore still had his hands on my neck, and his fingers ground into my spine as he pressed down on me. I was smack-dab in the middle of an angry hornet's nest of adults who wanted the truth.

I decided the truth would not fly with this group. I looked over at Jerry. He would not even look at me. He sat there, head down, looking at the floor. I knew Jerry's standard lie. He would just repeat over and over again, "I didn't do it."

My common sense began to kick in as I quickly analyzed my predicament. The teachers obviously found the pictures and took them to the office. The people in the waiting room were parents of the boys Jerry sold the pictures to. They thought I did it and now wanted to stone me. But what in the world was the chief of police doing here? Then it dawned on me. *This is a big deal and I am going to jail,* I thought.

As the tension intensified, everyone in the waiting room chattered and hollered all at the same time. There was so much confusion the chief bellowed, "Shut up!" He said it again, this time with more power and authority, "Shut up!" Everyone followed his order and quieted down. "I will take Jack into another room and make him talk," the chief said.

I had seen this in a movie. The good sheriff takes out his giant pistol and beats the stuffin' out of the bad boy. I was the bad boy in this scene, and I knew I was about to get it. The chief scooped up all the pictures, and on the way to the room where I would receive my beating I got a serious lecture about reform school.

If I don't talk, I am going to the big house, I thought to myself. I had heard this line before. This time, I believed it. The chief of police took me to the mop room. It smelled musty, mildewy, just bad. It had no air conditioning, just a light bulb in the ceiling and an old wooden chair. It dawned on me I had better tell the chief the truth or I could die in there. He put his hand on his gun and said, "I want the truth and nothing but the truth."

I cracked like a three-pound ostrich egg getting hit with a twenty-pound hammer. Truth gushed out of me like Old Faithful erupting at Yellowstone National Park. I could not stop. I am not a Catholic, and I had never confessed before, but I got on a roll.

"At Easter time when I was little, I stole Easter eggs from my sisters' baskets when they bent over to pick up another egg," I gushed. "I stole so many I won first prize and a big chocolate rabbit. Okay, I didn't really win it; I stole it.

"At seven, if my sisters gave me any trouble I hid their dolls. Doll-knapping became my specialty. At eight, a neighbor girl ran over me with her bike. The next day I got my dad's horsewhip and hit her with it."

The chief was turning red all over. His eyes looked like they would pop right out. Sweat dripped from his forehead. I sensed he was about to explode. But I had never admitted my transgressions before and it felt so good.

"You're an idiot!" the chief cried, halting me in mid-confession. "I just want to know about the pictures. That's it!"

Okay, now was that necessary? I thought. Being called an idiot took some of the joy out of my confession. Finally, I got to the subject of the forbidden pictures, took a deep breath, and began.

"Well, here goes," I started. "First of all, those are not my sisters."

I told the whole story from the beginning. The chief listened intently and kept telling me to look him in the face.

I kept talking. "Well, that's it," I said.

The chief then asked me if I knew what the sin of omission was.

"Not a clue," I said.

He said if I left anything out, he would get me.

"I told you the truth," I said. "You've got to believe me. I did not sell any of the pictures to anyone."

I think he believed me, and we returned to the principal's office. Wonder of wonders, with no beating and all my faculties (and body parts) intact. I sat in the office all day. Jerry and the Chief disappeared. One by one, others were called in. The Chief got most of the truth out of Jerry. Then he called us in together. Our stories matched and I was free to go. That day was the last time I ever saw Jerry. He was sent to juvenile detention. A short time later, he went to prison for robbing a convenience store.

Remember, a secret of success is that learning from our experiences, both positive and negative, makes us more efficient and effective. I began to learn from the predicaments Jerry and I got into. Sadly, Jerry never did.

I thought back to another time when Jerry and I were at the beach during a red tide, a harmful algae outbreak that kills fish and other sea creatures and makes the local beaches smell terrible. We were walking along the shore and there were dead fish everywhere.

"I have an idea," Jerry said. "Let's use this fish." He picked up a twenty-five-pound fish, smelled it, and said, "It's okay."

"What are you doing, Jerry?" I asked.

"We are going to be on TV," he replied. This big, slimy fish was so heavy we could barely pick it up. But we lugged it over to my motor scooter, and the three of us got on. The next thing I know, we were on live TV and I was listening to Jerry tell how he landed this big fish. The story even made the local newspaper.

As I listened and watched, I thought of all the things Jerry and I had done. Trouble followed whenever we were together. Like the time we skipped school and went to the state fair. Principal Moore just happened to be watching a broadcast about the fair on television and actually saw Jerry and me entering the fairgrounds instead of being in school. Be sure your sins will find you out. We got five whacks for that one.

I decided I didn't want to end up where Jerry went. My friendship with Jerry cost me my reputation. My own choices to participate in his grand schemes didn't help. After the pornographic pictures incident, my friends' parents told them to stay away from me. I was the boy who sold dirty pictures, even though I never sold any. After those naked pictures passed through the school, you would have thought I was Jack the Ripper, not Jack Arrington. I learned then the truth of the old saying, "You are known by the company you keep." It was time to start using the common sense I had, to change my thinking and my behaviors to match the motivation and drive I instinctively had.

But I still had a hard row to hoe ahead of me. Fast-forward almost two years from my antics with Jerry, and I was standing in front of Principal Goldberg, getting kicked out of high school permanently as a sixteen-year-old sophomore. No one in the educational system thought I had what it took to learn or be a success. My escapades had given me the reputation as a troublemaker. It was time to correct my inaccurate thinking and make better choices. I determined to prove them all wrong.

Strike it Rich!

Success Secret No. 4: Learning from our experiences, both positive and negative, makes us more efficient and effective. We must be flexible and change our behavior or activities to improve ourselves and our situation.

Pure Veins of Gold

1. Be careful and aware of the reputation you are developing. George Washington said, "It is better to be alone than in bad company," while Thomas Paine said, "Character is much easier kept than recovered." The company you keep can taint your good name if those you associate with continually make poor choices.

2. Some combinations of friends make each other worse, not better. You might be a great guy, and your close friend might be a great guy too. But if you two don't act like great guys together, don't get together so much. If the people you surround yourself with aren't improving themselves and helping you improve, it's time to surround yourself with new friends.

3. Not every opportunity is the right opportunity for making money. (Especially if it's an op-"porn"-tunity, if you know what I mean!)

4. Be sure your sins will find you out. Nothing stays hidden forever, and the shame and deception you carry in order to keep lies covered up cause physical stress and sickness, hamper relationships, and block growth. Admit it, forget it, and move forward.

Plugging the Piehole

Success Secret No. 5: Personal development is the gift you give to yourself and your family. Keep learning. Always make yourself more valuable.

My first step toward success came with the fulltime lawn maintenance job I got when I left school. It lasted all summer, and then it was over. When the summer mowing season ended, the owner let me go due to lack of work.

I knew I had to have cash flow, so I started asking everyone for a job. My next-door neighbor waitressed at a restaurant called the Dutch Pantry. She told me they needed a busboy on the weekends. It was a fourteen-hour-a-day job every Saturday and Sunday, five o'clock in the morning until seven o'clock each night.

With my neighbor's recommendation, I went immediately that Friday to see the boss. I thought I was a shoe-in. He told me to show up the next morning at five o'clock and to wear a long-sleeved white shirt. Eagerly, I headed to the restaurant the next morning. To my surprise, three other boys were there too to vie for the same position. The boss, Virgil, gathered us together for training. The fresh bread and bakery pies smelled delicious. Virgil began training us amidst the hustle and bustle of the busy breakfast shift. First, he took us over to the spot where all the pies were cooling.

"You can have one piece of pie a day, but never, ever the coconut cream pie," he directed.

That coconut cream pie looked fabulous. It towered over the counter about ten inches tall, piled high with slightly toasted meringue and shaved coconut all over the top.

"You are allowed two free meals a day, but no steak and definitely no coconut cream pie," Virgil continued.

This reminded me of the story of biblical story of Adam and Eve and the apple in the Garden of Eden. We could eat anything we wanted, just not the coconut cream pie. This was the first time I learned there was such a thing as company benefits. I was excited. Free food! But no coconut cream pie.

The four of us followed Virgil through the swinging service doors into the dining room of the restaurant. He sat us down together and began to talk real fast, drumming into us the importance of taking care of the customers. He instructed us to say, "Yes, Ma'am," and, "No, Ma'am." I learned how important customer service was from him. I learned good customer service meant more money immediately in tips for me. I learned not to curse anymore and cleaned up my language. He went on and on about how to present ourselves in front of customers. I drank it all in.

"You take care of them, and they will take care of you," he said.

He explained how to perform the job of busboy. It was not glamorous, just good, honest work. Our job description was as follows: Take trays of food out to the tables for the waitresses, fill water glasses with water or coffee cups with coffee, and clean up the tables after the customer leaves. Get the table sparkling clean as fast as possible. This job taught me the importance of cleanliness and organization.

I then asked the boss what the salary was.

"The job pays thirty-five cents an hour," Virgil said.

At that point two of the boys jumped up and left.

Good, I thought. *Only one left and the job is mine.*

I may not have flourished in school, but I did see each job as a learning opportunity. This stood me in good stead as I climbed the ladder of success. Remember, don't be afraid of hard work. Be thankful for the new opportunity. Study those in positions above you in every job you get.

The economy was in a recession at this time and jobs were scarce. After the two boys were gone, Virgil began talking about splitting tips with the waitresses. This got my attention. When I was younger, I worked at a Christmas tree lot for my uncle. I made more money in tips than my uncle paid me for working the lot. I had also seen the value of tips in the lawn maintenance business. If wages are like pie, tips were like the meringue piled high on that coconut cream we were not allowed to devour.

I got the job. I thought my first day at the restaurant would be a cakewalk (or maybe I should say a pie-walk). I had two waitresses to help with sixteen tables. My waitress partner Alice, who was born in southern Georgia, began with her version of training – hollering and slapping the back of my head. She would do this every time I cursed. "Only stupid people curse," Alice said. "You are smarter than that."

It is amazing how fast one can change a bad habit through this method of behavior modification. Sometimes, changes for the better are accomplished through experiencing a little pain.

A busload of college football players on their way to the Orange Bowl stopped in that first day. It was six-thirty in the morning, and the restaurant was overflowing with people waiting to be seated. It seemed like complete chaos to me. I felt like a kid who got on the horse that took off in all directions. "Get the water," "Where's my coffee?" "Clean that table," "Who told you to do that?" "I need some salt." On and on it went. I was at full gallop back and forth to the kitchen.

I saw what looked like a hundred eggs sizzling sunny-side up. The chef grabbed two eggs in each hand and cracked them at the same time. He dropped them on the massive grill, lining them up with the others. He moved so fast I was completely astonished. I stopped to watch him do it again as my partner walked by, slapping me on the back of my head.

"Keep moving," she said. "The window of opportunity is right now."

What is she talking about? I wondered.

Later, I learned that Alice's motivation for working so quickly was her three-year-old son who needed his momma to pay for an operation or he would die.

I never knew people ate coconut cream pie for breakfast. Gosh, it smelled incredibly good as I carried it to the table. The aroma tantalized, as it wafted from the serving tray on my shoulder to my nose. I could see the clear beads of sugar like crystal drops on top of the meringue, the yellow custard five inches high, creamy and soft. *God, please don't tempt me like this,* I thought. I had to snap out of it and focus on work. I could never, ever eat the coconut cream pie.

I had no idea how heavy dirty dishes could be. We used big oval trays with rubber mats on the top. I weighed one hundred and forty pounds and felt like I carried five thousand pounds of dishes. To this day, I greatly respect food servers. We ran, ran, ran from six until about ten-thirty that morning when the breakfast rush was over. I never even stopped to go the restroom.

When the breakfast crowds died down, Alice stood at the server station counting our money. She motioned for me to come over.

"Here is your share," she said. I got twenty percent of the tips – five one-dollar bills.

Boy, I am in the money now! I thought. A dollar twenty-five in tips in that four-hour period quadrupled my thirty-five-cents-per-hour salary. I thanked Alice and asked her how I performed. By this time I could hardly move. I ached all over.

"You are really fast, but you're kind of stupid," Alice said. Let me tell you, she had a way with words. She really knew how to motivate a young man. *Not.* There was that word *stupid* again. This really hurt. I got very defensive and hollered at her.

"Then you need to teach me, B**ch," I said.

She grabbed my face with both hands, leaned real close, and said, "I cannot teach you fast, but I will teach you smart."

From that day on we were truly partners. I took the curse words out and got the "Yes, Sirs," and "No, Ma'ams" down. And Alice did teach me. A lot. Her tips were pure veins of gold. You can mine for this kind of gold in every situation if you watch carefully and listen more than you talk.

The main focal point in the restaurant, amidst a sea of tables, was a scenic fishpond about ten feet long and five feet wide sitting in the middle of the dining room. On my second day on the job, I was carrying what felt like a hundred pounds of dishes. The oversized serving trays were efficient for transporting multiple dinners but awkward and difficult to balance. The restaurant was extremely busy, and I was in fast mode. As I snaked my way around the crowded tables, my foot slipped and I fell forward. I launched an entire tray of dirty dishes like a shot put. The people nearest the pond tried to take cover. Ladies started screaming. Then came a big splash and the sound of glass shattering. The entire tray and its contents flew right into the fishpond. If it had been a goalpost on a football field, I would have scored three points for a field goal. Suddenly, as if on cue, chicken bones, globs of mashed potatoes, green beans, and chunks of bread began popping up and floating on the top of the water. For the goldfish, it was a seven-course meal.

The eyes of what felt like the whole world settled on me. I could see by their shocked looks they were thinking they had better leave before that busboy killed someone. In my panic I ran to the back of the kitchen and hid in the walk-in cooler. At sixteen years of age, this was the most embarrassing thing that had ever happened to me so far.

I had been in the cooler no more than ten seconds when Alice burst in. "Get your butt out here and help me clean up this mess!" she yelled. "Be quick, but not fast." This sounded like a contradiction to me but I tried to do what she said. I thought long and hard about that comment while I spent my first paycheck paying for all the broken dishes.

***

Because of the quick pace working in a restaurant requires, I learned to think on my feet and to plan ahead. Every time I entered the dining room, I tried to accomplish two or three tasks at the same time. For example, when I took a tray of food out, I never returned to the kitchen empty-handed. I always brought a dirty tray of dishes back with me. I looked at every table each time I was on the floor. *How could I be more efficient?* I asked myself. I carried a coffee pot in one hand and a water pitcher the other hand. I quickly learned that the more efficient I became, the more tips I made.

Tips are like being in your own business and making a profit. Profit is better than wages. As motivational speaker Jim Rohn puts it, "Profits are better than wages. Wages make you a living; profits make you a fortune."[2]

Success Secret No. 5:

Personal development is the gift you give to yourself and your family. Keep learning. Always make yourself more valuable

I worked with another busboy named Jeff, who often showed up late. One weekend, he called in sick. That left me with thirty-two tables to bus, twice the tips but also twice the work. It was chaos on steroids. The next weekend, Jeff showed up but was late again.

Now, Jeff and I talked a lot about the coconut cream pie. That weekend, we could stand it no longer. After the morning rush, Jeff took one of the forbidden pies off the cooling rack. My job was to get two glasses of milk, two spoons, and meet him in the huge walk-in cooler. Inside the cooler, I located a hiding place behind the fifty-pound sacks of potatoes. Jeff came in with the coconut cream pie.

For several weeks, I had been dreaming of this moment. My mouth watered as he rushed in. He held it in front of my face. It smelled delicious. It looked like a pie on the cover of a gourmet magazine. We dug in like two starving savages who had not eaten in weeks. We were stuffing our pieholes as fast as we could. It was the most delicious thing I ever put in my mouth.

Inside the walk-in cooler it was forty degrees, and I was getting cold fast. The small light on the wall gave off just enough light that we could barely see. All of a sudden, I heard the loud click of the big door latch opening. Light rushed in, and I could not see for a couple of seconds. When my eyes focused, Virgil the manager was standing right in front of us. I had a mouth full of pie, another spoonful ready to go, and pie down the front of my white shirt.

"What are you doing?" Virgil demanded.

"We are peeling potatoes," I answered in what I hoped was an innocent tone but was really my smart mouth kicking in again. Virgil planted his hands on his hips and said, "I am really disappointed in you two." He fired Jeff on the spot and told me to go directly to his office.

Does he have a big paddle? I wondered. Remorse kicked in and I began to feel bad about taking the pie. In fact, I was truly embarrassed. That day, I learned a lot about business. Virgil said he would give me one more chance because I was never late and never missed a day. He also said words that struck a healing chord deep in my soul. Virgil said I was quick and smart. He called me *smart*. He told me he really needed me. Despite Virgil's initial disappointment, he wound up praising me because of my hard work and dedication to the job.

The lessons I learned at the restaurant were simple, but they were pure veins of gold. Make yourself valuable to other people, work on improving yourself, and show up to work on time were just a few nuggets acquired along the way.

Virgil went on to talk about truth and its agreement with reality. He talked about trust and the ability to rely on another person. Virgil was a very intelligent man with a lot of common sense. I told him how sorry I was for eating the pie. That's when Virgil started laughing.

"It's a test," he said, "and no one has passed it yet."

"You're sick!" I said.

"I know, but it's so much fun," Virgil said and we both laughed.

Strike it Rich!

Success Secret No. 5: Personal development is the gift you give to yourself and your family. Keep learning. Always make yourself more valuable.

Pure Veins of Gold

1. Don't be afraid of hard work. Be thankful for every new opportunity. Study those in positions above you in every job you get.

2. Customers really do come first. If you treat people right, they will treat you right. Learn people's names and use them. Look people in the eyes. Put others first.

3. Sometimes changes for the better are accomplished through experiencing a little pain.

4. Keep moving. The window of opportunity is right now.

5. Be quick but not fast. In other words, to work quickly as well as efficiently, you must stay focused on the job at hand. That means to be mentally in the game and pay attention to what you are doing, even as you work quickly to get the job done.

6. Don't waste motion and time. Think "efficient" and you'll be more effective.

Right into My Lap and Upside Down

Success Secret No. 6: Success means nothing without someone to share it with. No matter how much money you make, you're not living if you don't know how to find love and keep it.

Success Secret No. 7: Opportunities are open doors to go through, but one must be ready and take them seriously.

On my first day at Disston Junior High School in Gulfport, Fla., I was the oldest boy in school and in a new school for the eighth time. The first day I scoped out my new territory. I picked out the lovely ladies to whom I would offer the pleasure of my company for the rest of the school year. I spotted Marilyn, then Nana. But the one that truly made me look twice was Kathy Denning. Certainly they would all swoon under the power of my manly charm. Okay, at that time I was exceedingly vain. I admit I thought I was God's gift to girls.

Remember, my first job was at the barbershop, where I learned important personal grooming tips. I learned to brush my teeth three times daily, wear cologne, and get my hair cut regularly. Of course, it must be a ducktail haircut so the girls could see me combing my luxurious hair. Okay, so this was the 1950s. Think along the lines of the movie *Grease*. I really did wear a black leather motorcycle jacket and very tight jeans. I was a smartass and I could curse like a sailor. Every girl's dream of a real man, right? Ha!

Kathy Denning was a cheerleader who was way beyond cute. In fact, she was stunning, exciting, and overflowing with enthusiasm. She laughed and smiled constantly. Man, could she cheer! Watching her gave me the old school spirit, if you know what I mean.

On the second day of school the students gathered first thing in the morning in the old cafeteria, musty and rank from being closed tight during the summer break. It was time for placement tests. I sat at the end of a table with my back to the wall so I could see everyone coming in. Students bustled around helter-skelter, looking for friends while trying to find a seat. The noise and anticipation were deafening, the unknowns of a new school year exciting.

Then I spotted Kathy bouncing through the front door, wearing that incredibly gorgeous smile. Taking the path of least resistance, she moved down the aisle by the wall. My wall. The one about three feet behind me. I would like to take credit for having my next move planned, but I didn't. It was entirely spontaneous. When she was about five feet from me, I pushed off the table, my chair sliding across the freshly waxed floor and landing against the wall. Perfect timing. Kathy fell across me, right into my lap, and upside down.

I grabbed her and exclaimed, "Looky here, I have a cheerleader!" I held her for a few seconds and Kathy was a good enough sport to laugh with me. Everyone in the cafeteria laughed hysterically. In that moment, I realized I was holding Miss Universe. In one instant, Kathy became my universe.

Success Secret No. 6:

Success means nothing without someone to share it
with. No matter how much money you make,
you're not living if you don't know how to love.

I was a fifteen-year-old punk. She was a fourteen-year-old
spunky, beautiful good girl. It was a match made in heaven. But
we had to go through some hell to get there.

***

My job at the restaurant was going well. I was making good
money, and Virgil asked me to work on Friday nights after school.
I felt compelled to accept. Frustrated, I had no free time on the
weekends at all. I had no social life. Kathy wanted me to take her
out, but my work schedule got in the way. Every week, I would
think of my beautiful cheerleader at the beach or at a dance with
other guys.

By this time I had saved nine hundred and fifty dollars in tip
money. My new goal was to buy a used Corvette so I could take
Kathy out on the weekends in style. I decided I needed a new job
where I did not have to work every weekend night, plus all day
Saturdays and Sundays. Jobs were scarce and difficult to obtain
for teens. But I just had to get a job with tips and new
opportunities so I did not have to work every weekend.

Then my brother-in-law told me he could get me a fulltime job at
a new grocery store that had just opened. For carrying groceries
out to customers' cars, I would be paid one dollar per hour, plus
tips. The store was closed on Sundays, and I only had to work one
night a week.

The store wanted me to start the next day, but I did not want to
leave Alice and Virgil shorthanded. I gave the restaurant a two-
week notice. To my surprise, Virgil offered me an additional
dollar per hour plus thirty percent of the tips if I would stay.

However, time with Kathy meant more. When Virgil realized I was definitely leaving, he asked me to write my own letter of recommendation. He said he did not have time to do it himself, and he would sign whatever I wrote.

What do I say? I thought. *Do I talk about how I never missed a day of work, how I always was on time, that I work fast and smart, how well I interact with customers, that I am always interested in learning and improving? Do I write that I always smile, that I am enthusiastic, always grateful for the opportunity to have the job?* I wrote something to this effect and took it to my sister so she could look it over.

"This is all true," she said. "Let me say it for you."

In an instant, I struck a pure vein of gold. I learned that good letters of recommendation are worth their weight in gold, and that you can often write them yourself and ask others to sign them. Many people would be happy to recommend but don't have the time to write your recommendation. If you write it for them, it's a win-win.

The excellent customer service skills I learned from Alice and Virgil helped me move to the next level into a better-paying opportunity. These skills helped me make a good impression on the store manager at the grocery store. I was quick, smart, and polite. The manager said I would get one dollar per hour up to forty hours, but that I had to work fifty-five hours a week. I could also accept tips.

The first week I only made about ten dollars in tips. I was a full-time stockman and a part-time bag boy at Publix Super Market. Each week my tips went up, as I learned how to stock my area quickly and efficiently so that I could spend my time at the front of the store taking groceries out for customers.

I learned from Alice that some people tip a lot more than others. Therefore, I should get to know the good tippers and remember their names. After three months at the store, I cleared more than fifty dollars each week in tips. I saved all my tip money for my goal: a Corvette.

One of my customers was a bank president whose bank was located just across the street. I made a point of getting to know him and opened a savings account at his bank. He shopped at the store regularly and was a very good tipper. By this time, I was seventeen and had almost fourteen hundred dollars in his bank.

One day, he started talking about stocks and how they could work for me. I asked the banker all kinds of questions. He was impressed with my curiosity and invited me to go to lunch with him. During that one hour, I asked him all kinds of open-ended questions, such as, "How can stocks make a person rich?" and "Should one focus in one area of financial investments or many?" The bank president talked about food and grocery stocks, energy company stocks, and real estate investments. He recommended that I purchase Publix Super Market stock, because one of the benefits of being an employee was the ability to purchase Publix company stock.

He asked me if I had ever heard the story of *Acres of Diamonds* by Russell H. Conwell[3] He told me that diamonds are all around me if I just open my eyes to see them.

To my astonishment, he then said, "I will loan you twenty-five hundred dollars, and you can purchase Publix stock. It will gain in value. Dig in your own backyard."

I laughed. "You've got to be kidding," I said in astonishment.

From across the restaurant booth, he looked at me real hard. I knew I said the wrong thing. He reached across the table, grabbed me by the tie, pulled me toward him, and said, "Never laugh about money again."

I never, ever forgot that lesson.

Making money is a lot of fun, but money is also a serious thing and one must be serious about it. This time, I did not laugh. If the banker was this passionate about loaning me money, and taking time to teach me, I would sure do it.

Success Secret No. 7:

Opportunities are open doors to go through, but one must be ready.

So I did. I bought Publix stock. During that first year, the stock made a two-to-one split. I paid back the banker in one year.

I kept saving for my Corvette. I gave one hundred percent at my job. I really was thankful for this opportunity to make a living and earn money. I worked for a wonderful store manager, Mr. Bishop, who frequently gave me a good word and encouraged me. When I was called into his office, it was always a good thing. I usually got a small increase in my hourly wages.

Mr. Bishop kept every job application of possible job candidates on a table behind his desk. There must have been three thousand or more. Every time I left his office, he would always point to the big pile of applications and say, "Remember, you are one of the best of the best." He made me excited to get back to work. Mr. Bishop knew how to lead and inspire others. He could have used the pile of applications to intimidate me. Instead, he used them to motivate me.

The dress code at the grocery store was a long-sleeve white shirt and a black tie. I had my tie and shirts cleaned and pressed at the dry cleaners each week. One time, I got the bright idea to launder them myself to save money. About a month later, a new employee named Tom and I were taking trash out to the dumpster. We found a can of cat food made primarily from fish guts. The can was bloated and almost round due to being spoiled.

"Watch this," I said to Tom. I took the can in my right hand and fired it at the empty steel bottom of the dumpster. When it hit, it blew up like an atomic bomb, sending a mushroom cloud of fish guts all over us. Thankfully, we were not hit by the exploding metal can but we were covered in rotten fish guts. Although they were hardly visible on us, they stank. We reeked of dead fish. We went to the bathroom and tried to clean up, to no avail. Tom and I were walking, talking, rotten, stinky fish guts.

This all took place at eight forty-five on a Saturday morning, my biggest day for tips. I took Tom to the aisle where the air fresheners sat on the shelves, and we sprayed each other with a can of floral rose. Now we smelled like rotten fish holding bouquets of roses. I told Tom to stay away from everyone, and I went up front to bag groceries. I tried not to get to close to anyone. It didn't work. The first cashier said, "Jack, I think you stepped in something."

About that time I heard the manager over the loudspeaker. "Jack, come to my office," Mr. Bishop boomed. I headed toward the office and spotted Tom standing in the hallway about ten feet from our boss. Mr. Bishop ordered me to stop before I got too close to him.

"Tom told me what you did and I believe him," Mr. Bishop said. He then told Tom to go home, get cleaned up, and come back. Turning to me, he said, "I always expect the best from you, Jack, and this is not like you. Never do it again."

After Tom left, Mr. Bishop continued. "I've been meaning to talk to you about your clothes," he said. "Your shirt and tie are wrinkled and sometimes looks dirty. What is going on?"

"I tried to save money on dry cleaning," I said. "I guess it's not working."

"Did your tips drop off the last month?" Mr. Bishop asked.

"Yes, Sir, they did," I said.

I learned from this that the first impression you make on a service job affects the money you make. Always look good.

"Now I need you to go home, get cleaned up, and come back fast because *I really need you*," Mr. Bishop said. I was relieved to hear him say, I really need you. From that day on, I always looked sharp because it meant more money and gave me more opportunities. The schools I attended may not have believed I could learn, but I learned plenty from every job I had. I put those lessons into practice with each new opportunity. You can too.

Strike It Rich!

Success Secret No. 6: Success means nothing without someone to share it with. No matter how much money you make, you're not living if you don't know how to find love and keep it.

Success Secret No. 7: Opportunities are open doors to go through, but one must be ready and take them seriously.

Pure Veins of Gold

1. Good letters of recommendation are pure gold. Write them yourself and ask your supervisor or boss to sign them. Many people are happy to recommend you but don't have the time to write your recommendation. If you write it for them, it's a win-win.

2. Always leave a job on good terms and in a professional manner. Give two weeks' notice. Ask your employer what he needs you to finish before you leave. Work as hard on your last day as you did on your first.

3. At the restaurant, Alice taught me how to take care of people. Listen, listen, and listen. Look them in the eyes. Use good manners, like, "Yes, Sir," and "No, Sir." Give them the best service, service, service.

4. Keep learning and growing. Figure out how to make yourself more valuable. This is a key to earning more money.

5. You never get a second chance to make a first impression. The way you look speaks for itself. (Remember: no stinky fish guts and, if you run a service business, dry cleaning is worth the expense.)

6. Start learning now about investments. Get successful people around you to educate you about real estate and the stock market. The earlier you begin to invest, the better off you'll be over time. The great mathematician Albert Einstein reportedly said, "Compound interest is the eighth wonder of the world. He who understands it, earns it. He who doesn't, pays it."

I Hope You Learn to Dance

Success Secret No. 8: Remember: When the door of opportunity opens you must be ready to walk through. Don't let fear stop you.

Success Secret No. 9: The door of opportunity should always be the right one. If it isn't, you will spend a lot of time cleaning up your own mess.

Growing up, both my older sisters used me as their "crash dummy" in order to practice learning how to dance. First, they pummeled me into submission. I learned how to fight off two screaming women at the same time and still picked up some pretty good dance moves. After about two years of this awkward sibling ritual, I found out that dancing was actually fun. All that practice made us pretty darn good!

About three weeks after my close and funny encounter with Kathy Denning in the school cafeteria, I asked her to accompany me to a teen dance.

She was only fourteen years old and I was almost sixteen. She agreed immediately. However, she told me that I would have to ask her parents. I tried to joke, telling her that I told her that I did not want to take them with us.

"You have an incredible sense of humor," Kathy said, laughing. One of Kathy's greatest gifts was (and still is) her ability always to say a kind or encouraging word to everyone.

Upon meeting Kathy's parents, I knew I had to turn on the charm. I would make sure I did not use any curse words. I would use all those customer service techniques I learned from Alice at the restaurant. I would display only good manners. Kathy's parents grilled me for about thirty minutes before I persuaded them to trust me with their little girl. In the end, I finally received their permission to take her to the dance.

I was the only student in junior high school who had a car. As I approached Kathy's house, the front door swung open. There she stood. She literally took my breath away. I was completely speechless. All I could do was grin at her. I escorted her to the car, opening the door for her to get in. Once I sat down, I gazed over at her again. My mouth dropped open but nothing came out. I was so overwhelmed by her beauty that I was dumbfounded. I could not stop looking at her and dreaming about holding her in my arms during a slow dance.

At that time, students were not allowed to drive a car to school where the dance was held. I decided to park about two blocks away and walk the rest of the way. My speech was so paralyzed that I planned to compensate by smiling often and showing her some impressive moves once we got on the dance floor. At the dance, she surprised me. She was an accomplished dancer who not only kept up with me but also showed me dance moves I had never seen.

Wow. What a magical night. I held Kathy close as we slow danced, gazing into her bright blue-green eyes. Her red lips looked like soft rose petals. She was so irresistible I wanted to kiss her while we were dancing. I felt captivated by the scent of her perfume and lost in the joy of her beauty. The evening was euphoric.

My self-imposed rule of no kissing on the first date started to crack. Then I remembered the advice I learned from the barbershop job. Smile all the time. *If she really likes me*, I thought to myself, *she will want me even more the next time if I don't kiss her tonight*. But it was going to take an enormous amount of self-control. In fact, it took all the intestinal fortitude I could muster not to kiss her. The night flew by so quickly that before I realized it, the band was playing the closing song, "Goodnite, Sweetheart, Goodnite."[4]

As we left the dance and walked to the car, it was so dark I took Kathy's hand and held it. She leaned against me. I reminded myself that she was only fourteen, yet her beauty was far beyond that of a young teen. When we got into the car, she slid over next to me and told me what a wonderful time she had. I could tell she wanted a goodnight kiss.

On the way home, Kathy asked me questions about my life. She wanted to get to know the real me. When we arrived at her front porch, she stepped up one step and turned to look at me. I almost drowned in the aquamarine pools of her eyes. I told her what a great time I had with her. Then I leaned in and gave her a long hug. As I stepped back, I surprised myself by not kissing her. I said, "Good night, Sweetheart, good night," and waved goodbye.

I was suddenly thankful that my sisters made me learn how to dance.

***

About this time, we got a new restaurant in town: Morrison's Cafeteria. Kathy grew up almost impoverished so dinner in a restaurant was a privilege and a special treat. I mean, it was a huge experience. I took her to Morrison's, and it was her first time to see a cafeteria-style restaurant. As we stood in line, I could see her eyes growing bigger and bigger. She had never seen this much food or so many choices of food. She asked me what to do. I gave her a tray and told her to take whatever she wanted.

Everything looked delicious. The bright lights on the long serving line showed off all kinds of delectable treats. The aroma coming from the buffet filled our nostrils with intoxicating flavors. First along the buffet line sat the desserts. Kathy took me at my word. She picked chocolate cake, apple pie, vanilla pudding, and Jell-O and put them on her tray. We had only gone about six feet and had another fifty feet to go. At this rate, we would need about five more trays!

However, it was great fun watching her decide what to take. This was like Christmas, only with food. By the end of the line, she had selected twelve dishes of food.

"This is really a lot of fun," she said, looking up at me with a big smile.

Success Secret No. 8:

Remember: When the door of opportunity opens you must be ready to walk through. Don't let fear stop you.

A busboy delivered the trays to a table and unloaded all the dishes as we sat down. I tipped him extra because there were more trays than normal for two people. I had five dishes of food on my tray and Kathy had twelve. Realizing this, she then proceeded to ask me if I was hungry.

"Do you think I got too much?" she asked.

"Not at all," I replied. "I want you to enjoy this first experience."

About a half-hour later, Kathy sat back. "I can't eat any more," she said. "I put too much on my tray. Can you eat the rest?"

I told her I had plenty. Kathy then told me her parents were Catholic and made her eat everything on her plate at home. They told her there were children in China starving to death. Therefore, she should be grateful for any food set before her and eat it all.

"Jack, I will feel so guilty if I don't eat all this food," Kathy said. "What will I do?"

"Sweetheart, I have good news," I reassured her. "God is not nervous and will not condemn you for leaving some food behind."

Kathy laughed, looking extremely relieved. She looked at me like I hung the sun and the moon. And you know what? I think I could have that day. For Kathy, I'd do anything. Kathy and I got more serious over the next year of dating, closer than I'd ever been to anyone.

Then my ego got in the way.

I made a huge mistake and almost lost my Miss Universe for good.

***

I was still working at Publix, and every Saturday morning about eleven o'clock, this gorgeous girl and her mother would come into the grocery store. All the young men would follow her and her mother around the store, trying to remain unnoticed

They would run through the back hallways to beat this girl and her mother to the produce area where there was a one-way glass that employees could see through but the customers could not. This indescribably beautiful and voluptuous girl would bend over and reach into the shelves for lettuce. The guys would shove each other out of the way to get a better look. Every week, this happened.

While I stayed up front to make extra money, the other guys followed her around. She was so lovely. No young man could talk to her without stuttering and drooling all over himself.

One day after she left the store, a stockman named Paul confessed to me that he was in love with her. "Do you know her name?" he asked.

Now, I knew her name because I would take out their groceries. "Her name is Sophia and she is a beauty queen," I said.

"I can't talk to her, but you can," Paul said. "Ask her out for me."

"You have got to be kidding, Paul," I said.

"No, I am serious," Paul said. "I'll pay you to get me a date with her."

"How much?" I asked.

"Ten dollars," Paul said.

"Okay," I said. "Give me six weeks."

That next Saturday, right on schedule, here Sophia and her mother came. My plan was to get to know the mother better. I knew she liked me because I was very helpful and polite. I always used good manners like, "Yes, Ma'am" and "Thank you." I knew she liked me because she always gave me a generous tip. In addition to talking to her mother, I also started talking to Sophia.

It was a good thing that I had a stunning, cheerleader girlfriend, because Sophia was starving for attention. Two more Saturdays passed as I worked my plan. On the third week, after talking to the women and putting their groceries in the car, the mother asked me if I would escort her daughter to the Suncoast Beauty Pageant Gala.

I was stunned. "I-I already have a girlfriend," I stuttered.

"We just need you to be her escort for the evening," Sophia's mother said. "We will have our tailor fit you with a tuxedo and you can drive my Cadillac. It's a sit-down, formal dinner and my husband and I will pay for everything."

Can you believe this? I thought. They asked me to take her out and they are paying for everything.

Before I realized what I was doing, I agreed to the date. I skipped and ran back to the store to tell Paul my good news.

Success Secret No. 9:

The door of opportunity should always be the right one. If it isn't, you will spend a lot of time cleaning up your own mess.

To say he was not thrilled is an understatement. I was supposed to get Sophia to go out with him. Paul thought I must be kidding him. "You already have a gorgeous girlfriend," he reminded me. "One is enough."

I temporarily forgot the lie we told the bus driver about my younger cousin Gary's age. "Seven! Seven! Seven!" humiliated me so much I thought I would always hear it and never again tell a lie. I had learned my lesson good way back then. Or had I? Evidently. I was going to have to learn it all over again.

I took Sophia to the gala. I did not tell Kathy.

Sophia was a vision in her red evening gown, a white sash with "Miss St. Petersburg" draped across the front. I was truly a fish out of water. As we arrived downtown at the St. Petersburg Coliseum where the event was being held, I started to park in the back parking lot.

Sophia protested. "No, not there. Go to the front of the building and the valet will park the car."

"What's a valet?" I asked.

"Just go to the front," she said.

I drove around the block to get in line for valet parking. The closer I got to the front steps, the more I realized that this event was a really big deal. There were bright lights and a large crowd of people standing along a red carpet. I had my window down when I heard one of the photographers holler, "There she is."

I stopped the car and two men in short red jackets opened the doors at the same time. *This must be what it's like at a Hollywood premiere,* I thought. I sat there mesmerized, just looking around.

"Sir, you can get out now," the valet said. During the course of my entire life I had never been called "Sir." I was around eighteen. I didn't feel like a "Sir." But I learned that when a man is wearing a tuxedo and driving a new Cadillac, that man qualifies as a "Sir."

Sophia took my arm as we stepped onto the red carpet. She looked at me and quietly whispered, "Jack, you've got to smile." Ten or twelve photographers and cameramen surrounded us, taking pictures and interviewing her.

As we walked in, I turned to Sophia. "Who are all those people?"

"Newspaper and TV reporters," she said.

It hit me then like a ton of bricks. Kathy was going to find out. *Oh no, what have I done?* I thought. By this time, I really believed Kathy truly the love of my life. This could destroy our relationship.

All night long, Sophia kept telling me to smile. As I escorted her across the stage, all I could think about was Kathy. This should have been one of the best experiences of my life, but I just wanted it over with.

On the way home, Sophia chattered excitedly. "I want to be Miss Florida, then Miss America, and maybe Miss Universe and go to college," she said, revealing her dreams. "Jack, what do you want to do with your life? What are your goals?"

"I want to buy a used Corvette and make lots of money," I said. On our way to her house, I noticed her staring at me. I started thinking, *Great! This is the best I have ever looked in my life.* I had a new haircut, a tailor-made black tuxedo, and a touch of Old Spice cologne on my face. I smelled really good. As Sophia continued to talk about herself, I could see her face in the corner of the rearview mirror. She was truly beautiful.

Then I noticed her removing her lipstick. *Oh, no!* I thought. Now I am not the smartest boy in the sandbox, but I could tell she wanted me to kiss her good night. I remembered my self-imposed rule never to kiss a girl on the first date. I tried to think about Kathy. When we got to Sophia's house, I quickly jumped out of the driver's side and ran around the car to let her out.

I took my date by the hand and walked up the long sidewalk to the front door, her beautiful full gown flowing in the night breeze. One step up to the front porch, then she turned around and moved forward to face me. Miss St. Petersburg was just one foot away from my face. She was still chattering about herself and thanking me for taking her. Her perfume filled my senses. She smelled incredible.

At that moment, she leaned forward, her green eyes unbelievably captivating as she slowly blinked and looked right into my eyes. She had the longest eyelashes I had ever seen, slowly sweeping them up and down. The blush on her cheeks reminded me of creamy, fresh, homemade strawberry ice cream. Her face looked so sweet. My mind raced.

If I am not going to kiss her, maybe I could just lick her face? Good grief! Where in the world did that thought come from? I was losing all sense of reality. That's when I knew I had to get out of there. And fast. I looked down at Sophia's sash.

"Miss St. Petersburg," I said, suddenly grabbing her right hand and pumping it up and down like I was running for mayor. "Good night. I've-I've got to go." I turned around and never looked back.

I could not trade Miss Universe for Miss St. Petersburg. No matter how good Miss St. Petersburg looked or smelled. I came to my senses just in time, but the damage was already done. The following morning, Miss St. Petersburg and her escort were featured in all the local newspapers and television news coverage. This caused a lot of heartache and grief. I broke Kathy's trust.

Sometimes things look good, but they end in disaster. Make sure you learn from every experience, both good and bad. Then never repeat the bad.

I could have lost Kathy over this, but she was a strong young woman who really loved me. She always wanted what was best for me. She forgave me, but it took a long time to win back her trust.

Strike It Rich!

Success Secret No. 8: Remember: When the door of opportunity opens you must be ready to walk through. Don't let fear stop you.

Success Secret No. 9: The door of opportunity should always be the right one. If it isn't, you will spend a lot of time cleaning up your own mess

Pure Veins of Gold

1. I am really thankful my sisters made me learn how to dance. If you don't know how to dance, take lessons. Once learned, this skill will be with you for the rest of your life. Acting like a wallflower, saying, "No, I don't dance," will cost you hours of fun and joyous memories.

2. Practice encouraging others. Kathy has always been great at this. Before you speak to or about someone else, ask yourself, "Will my words HEAL?" HEAL stands for Helpful, Encouraging, Affirming, Loving. If what you are about to say won't heal, keep it to yourself.

3. Be an open and honest person in business and relationships. One lie can take down what you spent years building. Once trust is broken, it is very difficult to rebuild. You can say you are sorry, but especially when dealing with matters of the heart, deceit is like driving a nail into a piece of wood. After the nail is pulled out, it leaves a big scar.

4. If you break someone's trust, put one hundred percent effort into rebuilding it. Don't get tired of trying. Become an open book in word and deed. Follow

through. Be present. Answer every question honestly. Be patient as trust slowly grows again.

5. Real love is worth waiting for and fighting for. Don't be easily distracted by someone who strokes your ego (or anything else!). Love that lasts a lifetime, despite all the curves life throws at it, is priceless. Nothing is worth more.

Gently Kissed Her Tears Away

Success Secret No. 10: Train yourself to habitually think in terms of accurate thinking. This is accomplished by considering the consequences of decisions before you make them.

Except for my misstep with Miss St. Petersburg, Kathy and I grew closer and closer. Then Kathy's parents discovered that I had been thrown out of school. She had not told them. They were livid. They talked to the school principal, who informed them that I could not read or write. Kathy's parents decided I was not good enough for their daughter. They demanded that she break up with me. They banned her from ever seeing me again.

By now, we were both deeply in love. This turn of events devastated us. Although she tried to obey her parents, within a few weeks Kathy broke down and called me. She proclaimed her love for me and said she missed me terribly. Her parents insisted that she date other boys. Some of the rich kids with expensive cars were now bringing her home from school and asking her out.

"What do you think I should do?" Kathy asked me tearfully. Before I could answer, she told me her parents were coming in and she had to get off the phone. "I love you, I've got to go," she said. In an instant, she was gone.

I was crushed. I began to cry. I hurt so badly that I could not stop weeping. I felt like I was mourning the death of someone close. The next few months were lonely, difficult, and so, so sad. That old saying that separation makes the heart grow fonder rang true.

I decided that I had to do something. I asked my friend Bobby Boyer to ask Kathy to go on a date and bring her to me. About a week later, my plan was in place. Bobby asked Kathy's parents if he could take her to a movie. They agreed and he was to pick Kathy up at seven and have her home no later than eleven o'clock. Impatiently, I waited in a vacant lot at the beach where we would not be seen. The minutes felt like hours as my anticipation grew.

Finally, I could see Bobby's car coming. I knew that the love of my life was going to be in my arms in moments. Kathy jumped out of the car, crying and laughing at the same time, running towards me. Her arms opened wide to receive me. As we hugged and held each other, the moonlight illuminated her beautiful face. Her perfume was a fragrance of pure romance. We cried and kissed in each other's arms. I could feel her quivering and shaking as the raw emotions swept through her. I held her face in my hands and gently kissed the tears away, telling her again and again how much I loved her.

Taking her hand, we started walking toward the beach and the sea. As we approached the water's edge, the moon shone on her lovely face. I spun Kathy around, enveloping her in my arms, and kissed her passionately. The night was clear, the stars sparkled like diamonds, and the salty sea breeze encompassed us. The sounds of the surf muffled all other distractions. We were in our own world, on our own planet. My muscles tightened as we held each other.

Eventually, we began walking the beach. Kathy turned to me and asked where we were going.

"Right down there," I said, motioning with my hand to the beachfront behind the Hyatt Regency Hotel where the cabana-style umbrellas spread out before us. As we approached, it was obvious that all but two beach lounge chairs and umbrellas had been stored for the night. The two remaining still had thick, comfortable cushions in them. The pool boy responsible for the hotel beach equipment was my friend. He left the furniture out for my special evening with Kathy.

Earlier in the evening, I had placed blankets and a cooler filled with drinks and goodies for us to enjoy while we sat on the beach. We continued holding and kissing each other as the waves broke one after another on the shore. The moonlight reflected off the dark blue water. The waves pounded the shore, then pulled back again, creating a perfect rhythm of peaceful serenity which added to the magic of the night.

Then my mind returned to a split second of reality. Had I hit a new low? I had talked my friend into lying to Kathy's parents. I talked Kathy into lying to her parents. I should have remembered my cousin Gary and that "Seven! Seven! Seven!" But I couldn't help myself. I loved her so much. Kathy and I met each month for the next three months until Bobby said he was not going to be our cover anymore.

Success Secret No. 10:

Train yourself to habitually think in terms of accurate thinking. This is accomplished by considering the consequences of decisions before you make them.

Six weeks went by, and then Kathy called to say that the following Saturday she was babysitting some children in their home. I could meet her there at nine thirty after she put the children to bed. We could spend time together and talk. When Saturday night came, I parked my car two blocks away and walked over to the house, softly knocking on the back door. Kathy opened the door and literally leaped into my arms. She felt unbelievably good as I told her how much I missed her. I closed the door and began kissing her again.

Then I felt someone tugging on the back of my new shirt. I spun around to find a little boy in blue footie pajamas holding a dilapidated brown teddy bear with one eye missing.

"What are you doing here?" he said.

"I am making deliveries," I said.

"What did we get?" he asked.

I told him it was our secret and not to tell anyone. I handed him a peppermint candy from my pocket.

"You were kissing Kathy," the little boy then said. "Do you do that at all your stops?" He looked like he was only four or five years old, but he was asking questions like a state prosecutor. I suddenly began to feel sick at heart. I was begging this little boy to lie for me. *Seven! Seven! Seven!*

I told Kathy I had to get to my next stop while she tried to erase my visit from the mind of the little "Perry Mason" wearing the footie pajamas.

***

Three days later I received a frantic phone call from Kathy at midnight. The call woke everyone up.

"It's Kathy," my dad said. "Something is wrong. She's crying."

I grabbed the phone, my heart pounding. "Kathy?" I said.

"My parents are sending me to New York to get away from you," she sobbed on the other end of the phone. "The little boy talked, and I am in big trouble. I don't think I can stop them from sending me away. Jack, I will always love you, no matter what." Then Kathy told me her dad was coming and she had to go. The phone disconnected. I stood there a few moments in shock, as if I had been hit over the head and was trying to collect my senses from the blunt trauma.

The next day I went to Kathy's house to talk to her parents. I planned to tell them that I would leave her alone and stay away. They would not even come to the door. They let the dog Frisky out the back door so he would chase me off the property. Frisky was Kathy's dog and very protective of her. He was a black-and-white mixed breed, about twenty-five pounds of psychotic terror. Frisky was fast as greased lightning, with massive teeth and a very long tongue. That dog hated me.

I used to walk Kathy home from school, and when he saw me all the hair on his back and down his tail stood straight up. I instantly understood that this reception was a hint to let me know that Kathy's parents were not going to budge. They did not want to talk. They had no intentions of listening to anything I had to say. I ran like Superman, diving into my car and slamming the door on Frisky's head as he tried to remove my buttocks with his well-sharpened teeth. I put my window down and cursed at him. He seemed to enjoy the special attention and his barking only intensified. As he ran around the car, I pulled away trying not to run over him (I think).

The next ninety-three days passed without a single word from Kathy.

I felt crazy with agony and sadness. My broken heart longed for her. I did not know if she was ever coming home. Finally, after more than three months the dastardly silence was broken. Kathy called to say that she had been in New York with her aunt and uncle. Now she was coming home. She asked me to pick her up at four o'clock the next afternoon at the Tampa Airport and bring her home.

She wanted to confront her parents, and she wanted me with her. She said she was determined to have me. My heart leaped out of my chest. I could barely breathe for the excitement and anticipation of seeing her. The next day I asked my boss if I could leave early to pick my girlfriend up at the airport and he agreed.

Full-scale preparation began with a haircut. I selected a new, long-sleeve pink dress shirt with black pants and shoes. I donned a black leather jacket and gold wristwatch. I looked like a rich kid with a bad attitude. Next, I needed to create the perfect welcome so a trip to the florist for a dozen long-stemmed red roses was in order.

I arrived at the airport approximately an hour early, so I had plenty of time to park and get to the correct gate where Kathy would deplane. I purchased a magazine about cars to look at while I waited, but I was too excited to sit still much less concentrate on anything. I paced back and forth, staring through the terminal's large plate-glass wall of windows that provided a panoramic view of runways and taxiways. Then I looked over at the clock on the wall. Then I looked back through the window again, willing her plane to get there and park. It felt as if time stood still while my excitement grew. I found myself pacing faster and faster, like a caged bird longing to take flight. This was the longest hour of my life.

Finally, the plane arrived. I stood, watching it pull up to the gate. I frantically peered through the windows to see if I could see Kathy through one of the plane's port windows. No. No. No. Wait! There she is, seated in the last window seat in the back of the passenger cabin. I waved like a madman even though there was no way she could see me through the tinted glass.

The plane turned in order to position itself and she was out of sight. I walked over to the gate entrance where she would be exiting the plane and stood as close to the door as I could. Five minutes later, the double doors opened and out poured a sea of people. My heart pounded as I watched smiling couples embrace as they were reunited.

Finally. There she was, the love of my life. She glowed. Her skin glistened under the bright lights of the enclosed gangway. Her face lit up even more as she ran toward me. Her arms opened wide to receive my embrace. At last, at last, Miss Universe was in my arms. My loneliness began to fade away as I touched her, smelled her sweet fragrant self, kissed her, and gazed into her beautiful eyes. My whole world found peace once more.

All the time in the world stood still for us as the people around us seemed to evaporate along with the noisy clamor of voices and footsteps. There was no one on the planet but Kathy and me and the fragrance of the roses we were crushing between us. Slowly, she loosened her arms from around me. Tears of joy streamed from her beautiful eyes and ran in rivulets down her cheeks.

I handed her the roses and was going to say, "For the most beautiful girl in the world and the love of my life ..." when Kathy placed her two fingers on my lips and I knew to be quiet. She took the roses, smiled at me, and grabbed my hand as she led me away. I assumed we were going to retrieve her luggage. She pulled me along purposefully, as though on a mission. Her suitcase was the only one left in baggage claim. Grabbing the case, we went in search of the car.

Placing the luggage in the car, we jumped in and she slid over next to me. Looking up, still holding the roses, she said, "The roses are beautiful and so are you. I have been thinking of your kisses for ninety-three days and sixteen-and-a-half hours. Well, are you going to kiss me again or not?"

I turned, gently taking her face in my hands. I slowly kissed her forehead, then her eyes, then her nose with small baby kisses. Her eyes were closed as our lips touched and melted together in a warm embrace. The radio was on and Elvis sang, "Love me tender, love me sweet, never let me go ..." What perfect timing.

Kathy explained that she was supposed to take the airport shuttle from Tampa to St. Petersburg. However, she called me to come and get her because she was determined to get things straightened out with her parents and me. Miss Universe had changed. I had not seen this level of confidence in her before. She was determined and it showed. As we drove to her house, my self-assurance waned. Fear set in. What if Kathy's parents sent the psycho dog to chew on me some more? Her parents really hated me. The dog did too.

Upon arriving at the house, Kathy told me she would do all the talking. She asked me to get her luggage. I opened the driver's side window just in case I needed to make a dive into the car for a quick get away from psycho dog. Grabbing the suitcase, I followed Kathy to the front door while scanning and listening for Frisky. I could see my love's parents coming as I gazed through a small window in the front door. They had big smiles on their faces ... until they saw me.

Then the door swung open and to my amazement they invited me in. Kathy received big hugs and told me her parents were glad I was there. I thought I must have died and gone to heaven. I think her mom and dad even said they were glad to see me. *What in the world?*

Still astonished at this reception, I sat down in the living room while Kathy's mother offered us iced tea. My blood pressure was starting to come down, and I could feel my face cooling off as Kathy's mother started to talk. The first thing she said was that she and Kathy's dad knew Kathy was very intelligent, so they had decided she could now date anyone she chose.

"Your dad and I are sorry we sent you away," Kathy's mom continued. "We are sorry about the problem you had with Matthew in New York."

Okay, now my mind was racing. *Who the hell is Matthew and what exactly happened?* Later, I learned that Kathy's parents arranged a date via her aunt and uncle, and the date turned out badly. Kathy came back crying after the date, her blouse slightly ripped open. As it turned out, Matthew was not the gentleman he pretended to be. Although my blood boiled, I came to realize that two good things came out of this horrible incident. First, and most important, Kathy wasn't actually harmed. Second, I finally became a welcomed suitor. Kathy's parents knew I cherished her and would protect her.

After about an hour of talking, her parents gave their permission for us to date as long as I had her home by eleven o'clock. I could hardly believe what I was hearing. I knew then that miracles do happen and my prayers had been answered. Every man longs for a battle to fight and a beauty to rescue.

I had rescued mine. And she rescued me right back.

Strike It Rich!

Success Secret No. 10: Train yourself to habitually think in terms of accurate thinking. This is accomplished by considering the consequences of decisions before you make them.

Pure Veins of Gold

1. Try not to act impulsively. Think through all the outcomes and consequences as you plot your course of action in life, love, and business. In order to get past my failure at school, I had to think about the actions I would take to earn money. I had to stop goofing off. Unfortunately, I did not think through all the consequences when it came to matters of the heart. Our deception cost Kathy and me dearly.

2. In the instruction manual for mankind, a blueprint for men to live by, it says, "As a man thinketh in his heart, so is he."[5] Develop confidence in yourself. Post encouraging notes around where you can see them, on your bathroom mirror, on your steering wheel, everywhere you can. You become what you think about. Don't waste time thinking about bad things. The only thing you can change instantly is your own thinking.

3. For me, the definition of common sense is the ability to learn from one's experiences as well as others' actions and convert these into useful knowledge for one's life.

4. People will treat you the way you let them treat you. Hold your head high. Your skills are important. You are uniquely gifted. What you do matters. The world needs your contribution.

Miss Universe: More Than A Beauty Queen

Success Secret No. 11: You have two ears and one mouth. Listen, listen, listen and learn to keep your mouth shut.

Success Secret No. 12: Do things that you can duplicate.

Remember my goal to own a used Corvette? Well, ask and you will receive. One of my customers at Publix was a car dealer. Having a strong interest in cars, I asked him all kinds of questions while taking out his groceries each week. When I told him I was thinking of buying a Corvette, he said that was the best investment I could make.

Now I was thinking, I do not want an investment. *I want a Corvette because it looks cool.* After a couple of years, I had enough money to buy the car. My customer friend, who was a wholesale car broker, did all the negotiating. He told me that by paying with cash he was able to save me fifteen percent on the purchase. He provided an excellent service and only charged me one hundred dollars.

I made some interest in my savings account and used that to invest in the car. Four years later, the car was worth fifteen hundred dollars more than I paid for it. And that was after I put thirty thousand miles on it. I realized then what a good investment I made.

Life was good. But I knew it could be even better. I wanted more.

I wanted to marry Kathy. By this time, I was twenty. She was nineteen. We had been going steady for almost five years. She had graduated from high school, and we both had jobs. One night as I was kissing her goodbye, Kathy said, "I don't want you to leave me anymore."

As I drove away, *I thought, I don't want to leave you either.* I decided to ask Kathy to marry me. But I had a big problem. I still could not read or write. I was embarrassed. So I had hidden this from Kathy. I knew if I was going to marry her, I had to confess. No more lies. I had learned those lessons the hard way.

I will tell her the next time I am with her, I thought.

I was scared. I felt ashamed. With every ounce of courage I could muster, I said, "Kathy, I really want to marry you, but I have to tell you something about myself that you don't know. I cannot read or spell. I do not even know the alphabet."

"Jack, I already know that and I will teach you," Kathy said, smiling gently. "It's okay. "

I was so shocked and happy that I became overcome with emotion and began to cry. I had been hiding this secret from her for such a long time. I felt like I had just unloaded ten tons of weight from my chest. Obviously, this was not the fairy tale proposal like you see in the movies. This was real life. It was our life.

"Yes, yes, yes!" Kathy said enthusiastically. At that moment, I realized I would marry my dream cheerleader, my Miss Universe, and the love of my life all in one pretty, petite package.

***

During all the years of our courtship, I purposefully never took Kathy to meet my grandfather. Hubert Arrington either retired or was forced out of the moonshine and used car business. His car lot was mostly used to build high performance cars with hidden tanks for transporting bootlegged moonshine. They were known for being faster than any law enforcement officer that might have a notion to try and catch them.

In those days, the manufacturing of moonshine was not only illegal but also very dangerous. In the Ohio Valley, Grandpa had a reputation as a big man with an even bigger bad attitude. He scared me at times but I knew he loved me.

Early in his life, Grandpa sold the family farm and moved to Catlettsburg, Kentucky. There, he purchased an apartment building and a used car lot with three garages. In my youth, I would sometimes visit him for several days at a time. He would talk about business, and I would listen to him share about selling the farm and his moonshine stills. There was more money to be made in the transportation of moonshine than in the making of it.

I was about ten years old and loved to hear the roar of the engines. Occasionally, I would get to ride in the fast cars when he tested them for speed. I was told never to talk to anyone about what my Grandpa did. The only thing I could say was that we were in the used car business.

Despite his unusual and illegal profession, Grandpa taught me some of the finer points of selling. He instructed me on the "point of sale" (closing the deal), "never leaving money on the table"(Get as much out of a deal as possible, such as a commission on a sale or a car coming to you with a full tank of gas and full service, etc.), and chastised me occasionally, saying, "You did it wrong because *you did not listen.*"

I would never disobey Grandpa. My dad told me Grandpa once killed a man, but he also said the man was bad and needed to die.

I took this warning to heart. Whatever Grandpa said, I did. And I always said, "Yes, Sir." I believe these early experiences helped me learn the importance of listening, a skill that would serve me well as I got older. In business, you have two ears and one mouth. Listen, listen, listen and learn to keep your mouth shut.

Success Secret No. 11:

You have two ears and one mouth. Listen, listen, listen and learn to keep your mouth shut.

After I proposed, I finally took Kathy to meet my grandfather. I parked in front of his one-story, beautifully landscaped home. As we walked up to the front door, we could see that it was open. We spotted Grandpa sitting in his chair. As we stepped up to the porch, I gave Kathy a sign to keep quiet. We put our faces to the screen door and saw that he was sound asleep in front of the television, which was turned off. I could smell alcohol and cigar smoke. I looked over at Kathy, and she smiled at me. I lightly knocked on the door.

Instantly, Grandpa sprang to attention and hollered. "Who the hell is it and what do you want?" he said. In his right hand, he whipped out the biggest handgun I'd ever seen. Suddenly, it was pointed straight at us. We both jumped back.

"Don't shoot! Don't shoot! It's Jackie. It's Jackie!" I yelled. Grandpa always called me Jackie. In that split second I thought, *He is not getting an invitation to our wedding, assuming we make it through this visit alive.*

"Jackie, is that you?" Grandpa asked.

"Yes Grandpa, it's me," I said.

Grandpa lowered the gun and ordered us to come in. Kathy was visibly shaken but we opened the door. I introduced Kathy to him and told him we were going to be married. Then I quickly said we couldn't stay. We had to go. Goodbye. We hightailed it back to the car.

"He scared the daylights out of me," Kathy said as we backed out of the driveway, "but he certainly is colorful." That was my Kathy, the encourager. She always looked for the good in every situation.

On a Saturday two weeks later, we got married. It was a small wedding. I told Kathy I would make it up to her on our twenty-fifth wedding anniversary. The blessing of being married to Kathy was more than I could have imagined.

I had known from our first date at the teen dance that she was extremely smart. She had a quick memory, and I was convinced her IQ was exceptional. I definitely married up, if you know what I mean. She remembered every telephone number. Her English grammar skills were excellent, and she possessed a talent for writing. Be it business letters, personal notes, speeches, whatever, she proved to be exceptional. I struggled to learn my letters. Kathy was able to read difficult books like the Bible and understand them.

Back when she attended Boca Ciega High, the largest high school in St. Petersburg, Kathy was voted president of her sophomore class. She was only fifteen years old and the first female ever to hold a class presidency in the history of the school.

My cheerleader wife became my personal cheerleader. She was wonderful to me. We rented one side of a duplex and moved in. Just two kids in love. Making life even better, Kathy was a superb cook. I gained thirty pounds in three months. My weight jumped to about one hundred, seventy pounds. Since I was six feet tall, this was probably a good thing.

The duplex had a "For Sale" sign in the front yard. As I drove in and out every day, I noticed it. One day it dawned on me that I could buy the duplex. If I did, the guy next door would pay rent to me. I called the realtor and she said that if we had two hundred dollars for a down payment and a good job, we could purchase it. We did (have the two hundred). And we did (have good jobs). So we did (buy it). After collecting rent for four months, Kathy and I realized the tenant was buying us our first home. The rent covered the mortgage. We were acquiring an asset and the tenant was paying for it.

I was learning business Success Secret No. 12: Do things that you can duplicate.

Success Secret No. 12:

Do things that you can duplicate.

This is cash flow that I did not have to generate with my own time and labor. This first real estate deal helped grow the entrepreneurial spirit that had been planted inside me. Soon, it would grow. We quickly acquired a triplex, and the seeds of entrepreneurship began to grow

Strike It Rich!

Success Secret No. 11: You have two ears and one mouth. Listen, listen, listen and learn to keep your mouth shut.

Success Secret No. 12: Do things that you can duplicate.

Pure Veins of Gold

1. If you are going to make a large purchase like a car, save the money first. Pay with cash. You'll not only save all the interest you would have paid on the loan, but also you are likely to save on the purchase price.

2. Study the market for the best investment. If you are buying a car, buy used with low mileage. Also, buy wholesale.

3. In sales, do as my Grandpa advised. Focus on closing the deal. Also, never leave money on the table. This means to get as many "extras" as you can. If you are buying a car, make sure it has a full tank of gas or extra features. Negotiate for one more percent in commissions or get perks thrown in like a company car or extra expense money.

4. Think ahead and figure out what things are easiest for your customers or your bosses to give. Aim high, but know realistically what you will settle for.

Secret Entrance to the Exit

Success Secret No. 13: If you are not drawing your own lines, you are coloring in someone else's dream.

Success Secret No. 14: We are all salespeople. We have to sell ourselves and our dreams and ideas to others in order to be successful at whatever our passion is in life.

Success Secret No. 15: FEAR is no more than False Evidence Appearing Real. Don't give in to it!

While I was working at Publix, I met the man who would briefly become my first business partner. His name was Frank Grasso.

Frank was a college student studying marine biology when he got a job at Publix. My job was to teach Frank how to bag groceries and take care of customers. Frank was smart and grasped the training quickly. Over time, we became close friends. I was impressed that he was going to college and majoring in such a complicated and difficult subject. Frank and I spent lots of time talking.

During the course of our many conversations I explained to him how to make extra tip money quickly. I unpacked the meaning of cash flow, as well as how to make a profit. Frank, in turn, shared with me what he was learning in school.

Puzzled, I asked him how he would turn that knowledge into cash flow and profit. "I don't know," Frank said, "but if I get my degree, it should be worth something to someone."

Our friendship grew over the next four years as Frank pressed on to achieve his degree, and I became better and better at cash flow. I invested my money in grocery store stock, utility company stocks (electric and gas), and real estate. Frank continued to work at the grocery store part-time and we started talking about going into business together. Publix had begun requiring us to work more evening hours and Sundays. I did not want to work those hours anymore.

After earning his degree, Frank spent six months job hunting but found himself unable to obtain a position in marine biology. Finally, Frank received a job offer from the Lowry Park Zoo in Tampa. His starting duties would include cleaning the animal cages. He was told that perhaps after a year, he would be allowed to feed the animals. He would start at minimum wage for the first year. Wow! His four-year degree now qualified Frank to shovel animal poop for minimum wage.

Frank knew that this was less than starting at the "mail room" level at a Fortune 500 company, so he declined the job. After spending tens of thousands of dollars on schooling, not to mention four years of his life, Frank's higher education did not appear to do much for him. I spent those same four years of my life learning from experts how to make, save, and invest money. More importantly, I learned how to handle and "read" people, working all the time to improve my people skills. I figured out that other people were the keys to my success. Each day, I worked to become a better communicator.

I had seen how one of my first bosses, the lawn maintenance man, made money off me while I worked. I wanted a service business of my own, one that could bring in cash flow and profit without taking all my time and effort. During my off hours from Publix, I started my own lawn maintenance business.

Success Secret No. 13:

If you are not drawing your own lines, you are coloring someone else's dream.

Frank came on board immediately, and we began selling lawn maintenance term agreements, continuous agreements to provide lawn care for a specified timeframe. In our case, the term was an annual agreement. Term agreements generate continuous cash flow. To build a successful business, we needed to sell more lawn maintenance agreements.

However, as newcomers to the world of entrepreneurs, we got off track and started taking on landscaping jobs. We thought we could make more money doing both. Whereas lawn maintenance jobs based on a term agreement created cash flow, landscaping jobs did not. Once the job was sold and completed, it was over. No continuing cash or assets were generated.

We had no experience, so I spent time talking to nurserymen about how to plant shrubs, trees, decorative grasses, and flowers. I learned how to install new grass seed and sod. Frank was the salesman and acquired our first landscaping job. Frank and I were on each job early, usually at six thirty in the morning with all the plants and grass sod. We worked until seven thirty that night. After that long, arduous day, Frank visited the homeowner to collect our fee.

We started our day in the dark and finished in the dark. While I drove us home, Frank sat with the paperwork in his lap, calculating our profit for the day. I can still close my eyes and see Frank adding and subtracting costs.

"Well, how much did we make, Frank?" I asked.

"It does not look good," Frank replied. "I think we lost thirty-nine dollars."

In shock, I repeated back what he said. "You think we lost thirty-nine dollars? Is that including our labor costs?"

"No, it doesn't include our labor costs," Frank said.

"Frank, you have a college degree," I protested. "That can't be right!"

But it was.

Even though I was exhausted, I did not sleep very well that night. I had to figure out where we went wrong. I learned a big lesson that day: Stay with your plan. We went back to selling term agreements for lawn maintenance. For the next five months, we only sold lawn-mowing agreements. Frank kept looking for another job. He never obtained a job in marine biology but because he had a college degree he was hired into the management program of a major retail department store.

Now, I thought, *his real-life education begins: People management, salesmanship, Spanish, customer relations, and economics.* This was the entrance to the exit.

If you are college-bound, in college or have influence over those who are, I strongly recommend the following curriculum for you to succeed in future entrepreneurial efforts: economics, computer science, mental math, psychology, vocabulary, public speaking (including Toastmasters), Spanish as a second language, and effective communication skills. This is a pure vein of gold because I learned that we are all salespeople. We have to sell ourselves and our dreams and ideas to others in order to be successful at whatever our passion is in life.

Success Secret No. 14:

*We are all salespeople. We have to sell ourselves
and our dreams and ideas to others in order to be
successful at whatever our passion is in life.*

To Frank's credit, he reeducated himself. After working in retail sales and completing management programs over the course of about six years, he realized he had achieved all he could in that arena. Frank wanted open-ended opportunities. During those six years, he learned how to sell. Frank talked with me about real estate investing. He wanted to make money listing and selling real estate. He got his real estate license and during his first year was a leading salesperson at RE/MAX. The company paid no salary of any kind. Realtors made commissions from sales, and then paid the company for the use of RE/MAX office space. To survive at this company, Frank had to be good. To earn a good living and make big money, he had to be excellent.

***

As time went by, Kathy and I had our first son, Tim. We continued to manage the duplex and triplex. My job at the grocery store still paid pretty well, mostly from tips. But I was working sixty hours or more a week, from five o'clock in the morning to five o'clock in the evening Tuesdays through Saturdays. In the evenings, I tried to keep my lawn service company growing by selling maintenance agreements.

With my educational background, or lack of one, I had no choice. To achieve real financial success, I knew I had to be in business for myself. But I wasn't at the point where I could give up my "day job."

As usual, I talked to Kathy. "I am with you all the way," she said. Kathy handled all the bookkeeping for our real estate transactions. Now she agreed to handle the books for the burgeoning lawn business too.

About this time, fear tried to creep in. It had its icy-fingered grip on me. *Who do I think I am? I can't do this. I will fail*, I thought. Then I thought about it some more and realized I already had a small business. On Mondays, I mowed the grass at the duplex and triplex. I also mowed one of the neighbor's yards. The neighbor paid me ten dollars to mow her yard. Because of my past mowing experience, I could do it in fifteen minutes. A light bulb went off in my head. *This is good pay and very good profit*, I thought. The fear began to slip away.

Don't let fear paralyze you. It is like sitting in a rocking chair going back and forth and getting nowhere.

Success Secret No. 15:

FEAR is no more than False Evidence Appearing Real. Don't give in to it!

Remember in the beginning of the book when I said, "You must first have an understanding to have a revelation?" Well, my revelation came when I realized that my simplest job could become my largest and most successful business. As it turned out, it was. Arrington Grounds Maintenance Inc. was born.

Strike It Rich!

Success Secret No. 13: If you are not drawing your own lines, you are coloring in someone else's dream.

Success Secret No. 14: We are all salespeople. We have to sell ourselves and our dreams and ideas to others in order to be successful at whatever our passion is in life.

Success Secret No. 15: FEAR is no more than False Evidence Appearing Real. Don't give in to it!

Pure Veins of Gold

1. Only you know the burning passion in your gut, the dreams you want to achieve. Don't waste your life waiting to make them happen. Don't give up your life working someone else's dream. Learn, grow, save, and step outside someone else's picture to color in your own life.

2. Manage your time and money well. If you spend both too easily or in the wrong places, get help until you can practice self-discipline. Surround yourself with successful people. Glean all you can from them. Spend time with them. Read books. Listen to audiobooks. Success breeds success.

3. Remember that excellent salespeople never give up. They keep knocking on doors, knowing only a few of them will open.

4. Your first jobs should be ones that include tips. A job with tips is like a first business. If you live on your wages and save all your tips, this will help you prepare to own your own business.

5. Keep your current job while starting your own service business part-time. Be thankful you have a job and give it one hundred percent. This is good for your employer and teaches you how to be consistent in your own business.

6. Know your strengths and surround yourself with others who can complement them. If your strength is sales, find a good bookkeeper. Hire good workers. Stay focused on what you do best.

Ph.D.: Past Having Doubts

Success Secret No. 16: Begin with the end in mind and become an expert in your chosen area.

My goal in life became to expand my lawn maintenance business. Every new piece of advice I soaked up, every new business tip I gained was a perfect pearl of understanding. A jewel I could use to expand my business. I talked Kathy into letting me sell the Corvette and purchase an old 1959 Rambler station wagon. I used the cash to buy the Rambler and also bought more stock in the grocery store.

I had a push mower, a broom, a mower-blade file, a three-gallon gas tank and one paying customer. One agreement with the neighbor. But I was determined and optimistic. All I needed now were ninety-nine more yards to cut.

I planned to attract and sell one new customer at a time until I had one hundred customers. I would get off work from my fulltime job at Publix every afternoon and go to the best neighborhoods, knocking on doors to ask for their business. I asked each one if I could mow their yard all the time. I did not know I was digging into a pure vein of gold.

"What do you mean when you say, 'All the time?'" potential customers asked.

"All year 'round," I replied and launched into my sales spiel. I averaged three new customers out of every one hundred doors I knocked on. I figured out that if I knocked on one hundred doors a week for one year, I could have 156 customers. This would produce an excellent cash flow and grow huge assets for the business.

Side note: I recommend you watch the television series Shark Tank. It is fascinating to hear Mark Cuban talk about selling trash bags door-to-door. This show is a must-see for a person interested in starting his own business.

Back to Arrington Lawn Service. It did not take long to learn that the best day to make a sale was Saturday afternoon. I was getting better and better at what I would say. I learned how to brand my business.

My marketing strategy included advertisement. I always wore a hat and a shirt that said Arrington Lawn Service. This helped create instant credibility at the front door and visibility in my community. I was now acquiring five customers out of every one hundred solicitations.

At this point I realized I had to purchase bigger and faster equipment. I sold my Publix stock and invested in both a used pickup truck and self-powered mowers. I learned that buying a used pickup truck was a total tax write-off for the business. The lawn company and my real estate company paid for gas and insurance.

By this time I was really excited and exhausted at the same time. All I did was work and sleep a little. I had confidence I could make it happen, and Kathy was completely supportive. But it was hard. We now had two young sons, and Kathy was almost single parenting. However, we practiced Success Secret No. 16 and realized it was only for a season.

Success Secret No. 16:

Begin with the end in mind and become an expert in your chosen area.

With thirty-five signed agreements in hand, I was finally ready to run my own business fulltime. I went to see my store manager and tell him I was quitting. Up to this point, I did not talk at Publix about what I was doing outside of work. I just keep giving one hundred percent all the time I was there. I could see how this was preparing me to own my own company.

About halfway through my resignation speech, my boss surprised me. "You are the best employee I have ever had," he said. "You have always been so thankful to have a job and so smart with your time management here."

"You are smart and quick," he said. This was the first time he had ever told me this. He tried to talk me out of leaving and offered me a nice raise to stay.

"No, thank you," I said, but I was flattered.

"What about part-time?" He pressed.

I had not thought about this. I asked him if I could work on Fridays, which was a very good tip day, and keep my health insurance. He said I could. My friends Nick Damato and Paul Celli tried to talk me out of leaving, too, but I was determined to succeed in business. I finally gave a two-week notice. I was officially in my own business.

I kept adding accounts. In one year, I made four times the money I made before at the grocery store. Then I realized if I sold the business itself, I could make tens of thousands of dollars. This humble beginning led to a multimillion-dollar commercial grounds maintenance and landscaping business.

***

I learned quickly to utilize a few very practical perfect pearls of understanding to help begin and grow a service business.

First, start your own service business now rather than later. Continue to work at your current job, doing your best and always being thankful for it. Keep a grateful attitude, as you will need it to own and properly operate your service business.

Pick out a service business that genuinely interests you. Maybe it's dog grooming or window washing. Consider branding the company with your own name. Name recognition with the service provided is very important.

Have business cards made that not only have your contact information, but also outline what services you provide. Even in today's technological world, the business card is a marketing tool. It should have the main contact number for the business, your cell phone number, and an email address. It can also list social media. With a service business, you should include a good headshot of yourself, smiling genuinely and warmly. You are the business.

I can't say this enough: begin with the end in mind. After starting and successfully operating your company, you may decide to sell it. How would you determine the value? Start with written agreements. For example, let's say you have one hundred customers each paying one hundred dollars per month. One hundred times one hundred is ten thousand dollars per month. Take that times twelve months, and you're earning one hundred, twenty thousand dollars annually. Therefore, the premium for the sale of the company could be anywhere from sixty thousand to one hundred, twenty thousand.

If you are planning to sell any equipment or products in addition to the agreements, those items need to be valued separately and added to the total value of the company. These increase the value of the selling price. I recommend that you consult with a business broker about the asking price for the different types of service businesses you consider for yourself.

Check the prices of three other similar service companies in your local area to compare yours for competitiveness. Be the best, rather than always the cheapest, and charge for it.

Check to see what supplies are needed and their costs. Go to wholesale suppliers for the best quantities and prices. Take your business cards with you in order to purchase at wholesale prices. This is a must, as it will help more than you can imagine. Also, don't be shy about asking the wholesaler for assistance. Ask questions. He wants you to succeed because the more your business grows, the more supplies you will purchase from him.

If you open a window washing business, you might purchase buckets, hoses, a squeegee and cleaner. You may not need to purchase a business vehicle at first but simply operate of out of the trunk of the car you have now. Put your first investment into the tools needed to run your business. Purchase the best tools you can. Quality shows in the service you deliver.

Call every friend you have who could use your service. Tell them about the new business and ask them to please help you get the business started. While many people rely on social media, texting, and emails as their only forms of contact these days, old school personal contact works best in the service business. Pick up the phone and call friends faithfully every other month for fourteen months. Seven times is very important. Yes, seven times. Be consistent. Put the dates on a calendar and spreadsheet. Keep good records.

Learn by doing the job yourself. Once you are comfortable with the nuances of timing, supplies, scheduling, billing, follow-up, etc., then you can begin hiring employees to provide the service while you grow the business. Start with easier jobs you can do very well. Build up from there. For example if you start a window washing business, start with one-story homes. As you grow, then you can expand to multilevel homes, commercial properties, and more.

Saturday is your day to build your business. Go to the best neighborhood you can find close to your home. Have hats and T-shirts made with your business logo. Wear them when knocking on the doors of potential customers.

When they answer the door, say, "I am here to clean your windows," or, "I am here to walk your dog." Remember, you must be bold to receive business. If you try gaining a commercial business as a customer and they say "no," give them a business card and offer them your service the first time for free. If you are cleaning windows, stop and clean their front doors on your way out. You'll make a good impression and you just might win their business too.

Remember to greet people with a big smile. You are a budding company, and you must make a positive impression on the prospective customer. There is an old Chinese proverb that says, "If you can't smile, don't go into business." Take this to heart. It is completely true. After you clean the windows and get paid, tell the customer you will be back in two weeks. In this way, you build repeat business. Collect their information. Again, keep good records.

Be bold, brave, and daring as you are building cash flow. The more agreements you can sell, the bigger the company's assets and value. These are perfect pearls of understanding for operating your own service business.

***

After about three years selling one-year term agreements, I began to sell open-ended agreements at the one-year anniversary of the original agreement. I announced that at the end of the original agreement, there would be a three percent cost increase and there was no need for a whole, new agreement. This notified the customer of the change while eliminating the time-consuming and costly paperwork.

I did not realize at the time that I had tapped into a pure vein of gold. Most all service businesses are built on continuous cash flow and consistency of customer service. Once you decide on the type of service business to start, it is imperative to focus like a laser beam on the task of acquiring term agreements with customers. Term agreements generate cash flow. Term agreements allow you to build company assets with each agreement.

One more time: A service business based on written, term agreements equals a valuable asset that can be sold.

Kathy and I also continued to purchase more real estate. We formed another company called Arrington Properties, Inc. Incorporating the business provided the advantage of buying and selling single family homes.

Then we realized that we had a crossover business opportunity. Our lawn service business, which became Arrington Grounds Maintenance, Inc., began working for Arrington Properties. Arrington Grounds Maintenance provided yard and house cleanup services for Federal Housing Administration (FHA) repossessed homes that we purchased. This became a gold mine of opportunities.

I asked Kathy to obtain a real estate license, which she did, so we could purchase real estate and save money on the commissions. She is so smart. She quickly received her credentials, passing the test on the first try. Her intelligence, bubbly personality, and ability to competently multitask proved invaluable.

With two sons at home, she already had a fulltime bookkeeping job maintaining the business books for both of our companies. Now she began selling real estate. By calling all her friends to let them know what she was doing, she quickly handed out five hundred business cards within the first sixty days of getting her license. One month later, she became the top salesperson in her office and won a contest for having the most listings.

Overwhelmed with her success, Kathy came to me. "Honey, we have a problem," she said. She had taken on more than could fit reasonably into a normal workday. "What should I do?" she asked.

"Stop handing out business cards and stop calling everyone," I said.

Due to the giant wave of business she had created, it took Kathy about six months to work through it and get back to normal. We placed our home on the market, and she sold it in five days. The person who purchased it insisted on bringing an attorney to handle the sale.

The use of an attorney is not necessary to handle real estate transactions in the state of Florida. Most people use a title company. Kathy tried to explain to the gentleman that he did not have to spend a thousand dollars in attorney fees. Instead of being relieved, the buyer became agitated and upset. He stated that he would not go through with the deal unless he had a lawyer. Kathy agreed, trying to calm the man, and wrote the contract with the contingency of the lawyer's approval.

Thirty days later, everyone met for the closing of the sale. We were sitting in the office of the title company with the buyer and the title company representative when the lawyer walked in. He looked across the room and shouted, "Kathy, Kathy, Kathy!" He walked over to her and gave her a huge hug. It turned out that Kathy had previously worked for the attorney at a local bank where she once was head of the loan department. I looked over at the buyer, and he just rolled his eyes. Kathy is a joy and a blessing to everyone she knows and meets.

For our real estate business, we used billboard advertising as well as other printed media. Our advertising premise was that we bought houses and apartments in any condition. One day, I received a call to go see a four-bedroom, three-bath, one-story home in an upscale neighborhood. A very well-dressed gentleman opened the door. "You won't believe what I have in my laundry room," he said.

He walked me around, showing me the house, and again said, "You won't believe what I have in my laundry room."

As we walked into the kitchen, I could smell a pungent odor coming from the laundry room. "You won't believe what's behind that door," he said for a third time. At this point, I started looking for a means of fast escape. I spied kitchen knives on a cutting board. Okay, I have a plan, I thought. When he opens the door, I will grab a butcher knife and fight my way past the monster in the laundry room.

He opened the door slowly. There stood the biggest milk cow I have ever seen. He allowed this brown-and-white, big-eared, brown-eyed, thousand-pound cow to walk right into the kitchen. I was aghast. Here I was, standing in the middle of the kitchen in an upscale house in an upscale neighborhood, with a homeowner who looks like he works on Wall Street, petting a cow. The man did not look like the type who would know anything about cows.

I must be dreaming, I thought. *This can't really be happening.* "Do you know how to milk a cow? And can you tell me why you have a cow in your kitchen?" I asked.

"I was moving her to my new home in north Florida when my truck broke down out front," he said. "We live in a restricted neighborhood. No animals, much less livestock. I had to bring her inside until I get my truck repaired."

The real estate business provided many a funny story and strange experience. Throughout the years, Kathy and I have bought and sold more than one hundred and thirty pieces of real estate, both residential and commercial. We lost money on only three. The odds are in your favor if you become an expert in your area. To become an expert, you must study. Make every effort to present yourself as a proven worker who does not need to be ashamed. Speak the truth accurately.

In both real estate and lawn maintenance, Kathy and I were creating and acquiring assets. In Robert Kiyosaki and Sharon Lechter's excellent book *Rich Dad, Poor Dad*, the authors tell readers to purchase assets.[6] I totally agree. The beneficial thing about starting a service company is that your first customer is also your first asset. Plus, the cash flow generated from new customers becomes your asset as well. An even more beneficial asset is a customer with whom you have a written agreement.

Strike It Rich!

Success Secret No. 16: Begin with the end in mind and become an expert in your chosen area.

Pure Veins of Gold

1. You are ten times smarter than you think you are. Be willing to reinvent yourself. Be flexible.

2. Be on time and fully deliver everything you promise. This will help build your business by word-of-mouth and give you a good reputation. Priceless!

3. Make real estate investing a part of your future plans. Most rich people are in some way invested in real estate.

4. The four keys to being successful in the real estate business are wholesale purchasing, price, interest rate, and timing. Attend local real estate club meetings and read books about real estate investing to become knowledgeable in this field.

5. Read *Rich Dad Poor Dad* by Robert Kiyosaki and Sharon Lechter.

Oh, Happy Day! God Is Not Nervous

Success Secret No. 17: Always keep your word or don't give it!

Our businesses now ran well, almost too well. Each day was an effort to keep up. One time during this period of intense work to build our companies, Kathy asked me to accompany her to hear a very special woman who was coming to speak on a Wednesday evening at the church we attended. I placed the event on my calendar and promised I would be home on time. Then I thought no more about it.

The morning of the engagement, I got up at five o'clock in order to be at the office by six. Our trucks were already loaded with more than a thousand gallons of plants. The landscaping plans were ready, and I had assembled a team of eight men and two women to work on the job. The goal was to get this rather large project accomplished in one day.

However, only six of the eight men showed up for work. I was extremely disappointed because it meant that instead of supervising, I was going to have to perform the work of the missing men. As it was, we would have to really push ourselves hard to get the job done in a day. To suggest that I had a bad attitude is stating it mildly. At ten o'clock I was still complaining and cursing.

My shovel was flying as fast as it could when suddenly I received a quick kick in the butt that almost knocked me over. "I am tired of your bitching," my foreman Carter Phillips said. "You should be thankful you have work."

What a wake-up call. He was absolutely right. A bad attitude at the top "runs downhill" and quickly penetrates an entire team of employees. I learned a huge lesson that day about attitude and how a professional owner or manager should behave around his staff.

In spite of the setbacks, we got the job done. I was exhausted, not only from the hard labor but also from working for twelve hours in ninety-five-degree heat. All I could think about was how comfortable my big green leather reclining chair was going to feel when I got home.

As I walked in the door, my wife sweetly said, "I have your clothes laid out on the bed and we have to leave in thirty minutes."

"Where are we going?" I asked.

"Don't you remember? To church to hear Sister Sara speak," Kathy replied.

I was so stiff and tired I could barely move. The words "You promised" kept buzzing around in my head. I got a shower, dressed, gobbled down some dinner, and off we went.

The church was packed with people. We arrived a few minutes late, and the only place left to sit was down front, in the middle of the front row, directly in front of the podium. The stage lights were so bright I felt like I was on stage and everyone in the auditorium was staring at me. Our seats were only about ten feet from the stage and maybe a few feet below it. I flopped down in the seat. It felt so good just to be able to sit again.

A choir director came out and welcomed everyone, asking us all to stand. I did not want to stand. I was not going to stand. I couldn't stand. I had been on my feet all day. I sat there, enjoying my seat, looking straight ahead, hoping that Kathy wouldn't notice I was still sitting. Wrong! She leaned over.

"Jack, they said for everyone to stand," my wife prompted. "We are going to sing." After singing what seemed like fifty songs, I was finally allowed once again to collapse into my seat as the choir continued to serenade us. Suddenly, I got cramps from hell in the backs of my legs. I had been praying that the choir would shut up and go away. Now I shot out of my seat and began jumping around right in front of the podium. The bright lights illuminated my every hop. Every move I made seemed to keep perfect time with the music. The choir was singing, "Oh happy day. Oh happy day ..." and I was jumping around in circles holding one leg and then the other.

"Hallelujah, he has the anointing!" A man in the back of the room shouted. Kathy came over to me to try and get me back to my seat. The cramps finally stopped and I collapsed into my chair. I sank as low as I could down into the pew. All I could think about was how horribly I had just embarrassed Kathy and myself. I wanted Kathy always to be proud of me. But the night was still young.

The choir director motioned for everyone to sit down and began introducing the speaker. After about five minutes of glowing introductory remarks, I was expecting the Flying Nun to come out and make a few passes over the heads of the audience.

"Here she is: Sister Sara," he announced.

My first impression was that this tiny little lady was only about nine years old. She might have weighed all of eighty pounds and was about four feet, eight inches tall. She dragged a stool behind her with her left hand while pointing a finger toward heaven with her right hand. She wore a black habit and walked very slowly across the stage. It was so quiet, I could hear my heart beat. Finally, she got to the center of the stage and slowly climbed onto the stool. It felt like an eternity. Now I could see her face. It glowed like an angel. She no longer looked nine. She appeared to be about ninety years old.

Suddenly, the lights in the auditorium went out except for three spotlights silhouetting the backs of Kathy's and my head. They were aimed right on Sister Sara and us. I recall Sister Sara sitting on the stool for what felt like about ten minutes before she said a word. The auditorium went completely quiet and still.

I closed my eyes for a minute or two, when my head fell back and my shoulders began to list to the right. I opened my eyes just before I fell onto Kathy.

Then Sara spoke very slowly, "God loves you." It must have taken her five minutes to say these three words. Then she paused for another long silence that seemed to go on forever. She held the microphone close to her lips and said very softly, "He really does."

By this time I could not keep my eyes open. I was melting in my seat like a scoop of ice cream in the hot sun. Kathy poked me, leaning over to tell me not to fall asleep. I snapped out of it and sat straight up, my head in the spotlight again. Then I began melting away again. I put my head in my hands with my elbows on my knees and closed my eyes. Kathy was poking me again but I could not respond. I was so, so tired.

I could feel myself getting closer and closer to the floor. I remember opening my eyes and seeing a mirage of my bed in front of me. *I must get to it*, I thought. I slipped onto my hands and knees, onto the floor and crawled into my bed.

Now the spotlights were on Sister Sara and me, lying on the floor directly in front of her. I completely passed out, sound asleep. I vaguely remember four men carrying me out to my car and laying me in the back seat. I woke the next morning to the alarm clock, thinking, *What a strange dream!* I put on my work clothes and went to the kitchen for a cup of coffee. Lying on the table was a brochure about Sister Sara and a note from Kathy telling me what I had done. My only defense was that at least I kept my word!

Success Secret No. 17:

Always keep your word or don't give it.

Strike It Rich!

Success Secret No. 17: Always keep your word or don't give it!

Pure Veins of Gold

1. When you make a commitment, stick to it.

2. Show up on time. It is better to be one hour early than even a few minutes late.

3. When you promise to attend an event, especially when that promise is to your wife, make sure you are rested!

4. Google "The Time You Have (In JellyBeans)." In 2013, performance artist Ze Frank put together a little video that shows the average number of days any human being has to live. He demonstrates this number with a pile of jellybeans. He subtracts the time in jellybeans spent sleeping, working, doing chores, etc. As the pile shrinks, it quickly becomes clear how precious your time is. Don't waste a minute of it!

She Is Not Yours. She Is Mine.

Success Secret No. 18: Practice over and over in your mind in order to win or be successful. You must visualize success.

Success Secret No. 19: The most important assets are the human kind.

As I mentioned earlier, written agreements assure cash flow for a specified and continuous timeframe. The most important assets, however, are the human kind. About this time, I faced the greatest crisis of my life. My greatest asset in life lay motionless and unresponsive in a hospital bed. My wife, the mother of my children, my Miss Universe, was dying. Kathy was in a coma, suffering from phlebitis, with severe blood clots in her legs. We had been fighting this battle for months.

I always visualized my success when it came to business. I could smell success, see it, taste it. I practiced it over and over again in my mind. I saw myself a winner. I determined not to give up on Kathy. We would be successful in this grave medical fight for her life. It was not easy to visualize success now, but I would never give up.

Success Secret No. 18:

Practice over and over in your mind in order to win or be successful. You must visualize success.

I could not believe this was happening to my smart, beautiful, precious wife. It seemed like only yesterday when I first saw her at school. Throughout our years together, Kathy always amazed me.

She came to me one day not too long after we were married and said, "I am thinking of starting a weekly Bible study at the house. What do you think?" I told her to go for it. In less than three years, she was sharing the Good News with more than one hundred and fifty ladies weekly.

Kathy became active in an organization called Concerned Women For America, where she held the office of president for the Florida chapter. She was president over 43,000 members. After that, she became the national chairwoman, presiding over an organization that boasted 750,000 women as members.

One day, we received a call from the White House. Yes, *that* White House. President Ronald Reagan needed to talk to Kathy. She knocked my socks off. It was easy to see why Kathy was so important to my business success. She was my personal assistant, office manager, financial assistant, confidant and counselor. More than that, she was my wife, lover, mother to our sons, and my very best friend. It was petrifying to see her now, lying so pale and still.

This rough period taught me the value of time management. To survive, I eliminated reading the newspaper and watching television. The boys and I shared one glass each and ate from paper plates due to the lack of time to clean and wash. I learned that I could live without things I once thought were important. I also learned to prioritize. Business felt important, but Kathy and our sons were the most important of all.

One night very late, the hospital called to tell me to come immediately. I dropped the boys off at my sister's house and flew to Kathy's side. I fell to my knees beside her bed to pray. With my face buried in the sheets next to her, I begged God to heal her. I had been praying this for months. I stayed there all night. It finally registered that it was almost dawn, and I had not moved.

Suddenly, as clear as a bell, just as clearly as you are reading the words on this page, God said to me, "She is not yours. She is mine."

At that moment, Kathy put her hand on my head. When I looked up, her eyes were open. "You are the love of my life, and I am going to live," Kathy said. She had been suffering, bedridden, and in and out of hospitals for more than six months; but I knew deep within my heart that her illness was indeed over.

Human relationships are more important than anything else. Never forget: Your loved ones are more important than any business you start.

Success Secret No. 19:

The most important assets are the human kind.

Kathy loved Disney World, so within a week of leaving the hospital I decided to celebrate her life by taking her to the Magic Kingdom. It can be nearly impossible to secure a reservation at a Disney hotel with only a one-week notice. However, perhaps even miraculously, we were able to go (an added blessing from God). She was still quite weak, but from our room she could rest and still watch the night parade and fireworks on the lake. One evening when it was very late and few people were on the Monorail, I obtained the seats in the front of the Monorail for us. I held Kathy in my arms as we quietly rode the rail into the wee hours of the morning. The park was lit like a fantasy fairyland, and she loved the breathtaking views of the multicolored lights shimmering in the dark. It was indeed a wonderful time celebrating her life. Miss Universe was coming back to me.

After that weekend, I had to go back to work. The last six months of dealing with her illness and me handling the children and the housekeeping caused the businesses to really suffer. Had it not been for the help offered by my sister Bonnie, I would never have made it through the ordeal. If I wasn't thankful before, I certainly learned to be thankful now. Kathy's scary medical crisis ended, but the lessons I learned through it would last the rest of my life.

Strike It Rich!

Success Secret No. 18: Practice over and over in your mind in order to win or be successful. You must visualize success.

Success Secret No. 19: The most important assets are the human kind.

Pure Veins of Gold

1. Manage your time wisely and thoughtfully. Make sure you get the most important things done, not just the most immediate. Study some of the ways successful businessmen (and women) organize their days. Develop a time management system that works for you and stick to it.

2. Valuable lessons come with crises. When the crisis passes, remember what you learned. Crises sharpen our senses. They force us to slow down and to prioritize. In times of crisis, we whittle away the things in our days that have little importance. Hold these lessons close after the crisis is over.

3. Don't try to do it all yourself. When tragedy strikes, accept help from your community of friends and family. You can't be everything for everyone. Focus on the most important and delegate the rest.

4. Keep love alive. If you are lucky enough to have love in your life, celebrate it. Bring home flowers. Practice romance daily. Get creative in the ways you express your love. Try to outdo yourself every time. Never take your most precious human assets for granted.

Escape Into The Light

*Success Secret No. 20: Watch out for time wasters.
You only get one life, one finite amount of time.
Spend it wisely.*

There's nothing like a near-death experience to give you a wake-up call about keeping your priorities straight. Especially when you nearly die at the dump.

Let me explain.

My pickup truck was loaded to overflowing as I approached the city dump to unload. Ahead of me was a line of massive commercial dump trucks, some already emptied and others waiting to be unloaded. The noises coming from overhead were deafening, as thousands of seagulls darted about like savage beasts angling for their last meal. It was hot, humid, and sultry. What air there was had the pungent stench of baking garbage, compliments of the Florida sunshine on a hot summer day.

Finally, it was my turn to unload my small truck. As I walked back toward the rear of the truck, looking down to avoid tripping over the uneven piles of garbage, the driver of a huge city garbage truck began dumping his load too close to my truck and me. As I looked up, thousands of pounds of everything you can imagine (and some things you don't want to imagine) were about to rain down on top of me. I screamed for him to stop but it was too late.

I spun around just before garbage pelted me like an avalanche. The mounds of mess literally drove me to the ground, burying me and half of my truck. I was able to keep my body off the ground by bracing myself on my hands and knees. I knew I was going to die one day, but to be buried under tons of garbage was not the way I planned to go.

A few moments later, I found myself in total blackness, buried alive. I was able to take small breaths, thankfully, due to a small pocket of air. Thank God the driver, at the last second, looked in his rearview mirror and saw me as his load careened down. He quickly ran for help, grabbing other drivers and site workers who immediately began to dig me out. Hallelujah!

Out of the darkness and into the light and glorious air, they pulled me. My head came out first, then my arms, and then with more digging they were finally able to tug my body out. It was like being stuck in quicksand. The harder I tried to get out, the deeper I sank. All I could do was remain still while they dug their way through the stinking, putrid muck to reach me. As they picked rotten lettuce and potato peels off my head, I found myself reeking of fish guts. I was disgusting. But I was alive.

As I became the owner of many service businesses, it was easy to spread myself too thin. I loved success. I loved achievement. I liked my businesses. There were many times I was busy at work when I should have given more time to my family. Let's just admit it: Work can feel easier than relationships. You feel productive. You see the fruits of your labor more quickly and easily than you do the "work" you put into your spouse and your kids. Still, no work is more important than the "love" work.

If you are going to be a successful entrepreneur, you have to manage the time you have as if it is your most valuable commodity. Because it is. Watch out for time wasters. Before you play that video poker game, watch another television show, or surf the Internet or social media just for fun, ask yourself: *Does this activity add anything to my life and health physically, spiritually, emotionally, relationally, financially, or intellectually?*

Success Secret No. 20:

Watch out for time wasters. You only get one life, one finite amount of time. Spend it wisely.

If the activity you choose adds nothing more to your life than momentary self-pleasure, it's a time-waster. I would go so far as to say get rid of it. Maybe playing video poker relieves stress, you want to argue. So does going for a walk, and it's a lot better for you. Take even your leisure time seriously, to some degree. Make it count. Build memories with loved ones. Improve your physical health. Stretch yourself mentally by reading a new book or learning a new hobby or skill.

One way to see how you truly spend your time is to keep a time diary for twenty-one days or for a month. Write down everything you do. Everything. Note the time each activity started and ended. At the end of the period you've chosen, look back and add up the time you spent in each category – sleeping, eating, reading, working and all the other ways you spent your time. Those are minutes, hours, days, and weeks of your precious life that are now gone. You'll never get them back. Your "bucket" of time is a little bit lighter. Look for the ways you wasted your time. Determine to eliminate as many time wasters as you can.

One big time sucker is the internet. With all our phones, tablets, and laptops, we spend large chunks of our lives online. Of course, the internet can be an encyclopedia of information, a researcher's dream to help find just about anything and anyone. Business products, business questions, services, etc., can probably be found or answered using the internet.

However, the internet also can easily and quickly become an avalanche of garbage, drowning you in useless information and time-consuming electronic chases. It is easy to become distracted and sidetracked using the internet. To use this tool to its best advantage, you must manage your time when you are using it. I would go so far as to say you should use it only as the business tool that it is, not for entertainment.

I bought a new phone recently that can be voice activated. I spoke these words into the phone: "Local model homes." Instantly, pictures of local nude women models popped up, with full sound. Here I was, innocently sitting in a food court of a local shopping mall having lunch, and wham! People crowded all through the food court, all around me, as I frantically tried to clear my new phone as fast as I could. I pushed every button on the phone, having gone into a full-blown panic, trying desperately to get the pictures and sounds off the phone.

It went from bad to worse as pornographic videos now populated the screen. *How do I stop this thing?* I thought. I could not even get the phone to turn off. In my frustration and exasperation, I seriously considered smashing the phone against the table leg. Common sense prevailed, and I pocketed the phone and headed for my car. All I could think about was that I had a wife and grandchildren at home, and I couldn't stop this stupid phone from playing all that porn.

Off to the phone store I went. It was packed with customers. This must have been the day that no one had anything else on their planners except to go to the phone store. I took a number. Seven employees waited on people, six young men and one very young woman. As time passed, I watched the service representatives rotate to each customer, trying to make sure I did not get the young woman.

Ninety minutes later, I still waited. I determined not to leave before getting the phone cleaned out and back to normal. My number came up and I could see two of the male employees getting ready to help me. *Thank God it is not the young lady*, I thought to myself.

Then, just as I walked up to the young man at the counter, he leaned over to the other employees, declared it was time for his break, and walked away. I turned toward the next man, only to hear this service rep say, "Mary Lou, will you take care of Mr. Arrington? I have to go get new stock for the front of the store."

Helplessly, I turned toward the young lady. I felt like I was in shock as she smiled brightly and introduced herself.

"Hi, I am Mary Lou, how may I help you?" she said.

I could feel my face growing hot and turning red and then redder as I tried to think of what to say and how to explain my predicament. I could say someone stole my phone and I just got it back. I thought. *No, no. I could say my brother did it. Wait, I don't have a brother.* Mary Lou's next words brought me back to the present.

"Well, Mr. Arrington, I am here to help you," she continued. "What's wrong with your phone?"

"Well," I replied, "Well, here goes … You won't believe this, but I am in the real estate business and I have an app for voice activation. I spoke the phrase 'local model homes' into the phone and local nude models popped up."

I continued with my story until it was all finished. Then Mary Lou looked me straight in the eyes and said, "Don't worry. This happens all the time."

She immediately began the process of removing all the unwanted material. I was extremely embarrassed, but I think she believed me. The point of my story? It wasted five hours of my precious time. I was unable to get anything accomplished, including my goal for that day.

Time is the most important thing there is because it is life itself. When it is gone, you can't ever get it back.

Strike It Rich!

Success Secret No. 20: Watch out for time wasters.
You only get one life, one finite amount of time.
Spend it wisely.

Pure Veins of Gold

1. Buy a pocket planner or notebook where you can keep a time diary for the next few weeks. Record everything you do and how much time it takes so you can see where your time is actually spent.

2. Once you evaluate where your time is spent, look at the categories that are getting the short end of the stick. Are you getting enough sleep? Are you exercising? Are you pursuing anything intellectual that expands your knowledge?

3. Keep the main things the main things. Faith and family come before business. Yes, you want to be a success and provide for your family. But they also need your presence. It is a priceless gift to the ones you love when you spend time with them.

4. Find recreational activities that your whole family loves. Get some board games, go for family walks and bike rides, let the kids put on a show for you, hold your partner's hand, and watch sunsets together.

The Ice Box Ate Me

Success Secret No. 21: Look for the humor in every situation. Then figure out what you can learn from it.

One time back when my kids were still young, we stopped at a convenience store to pick up a ten-pound bag of ice for our cooler. My wife and sons were with me in the pickup truck with our new boat in tow. Everyone was excited about spending the day on the water, especially me. I jumped out of the truck and sprinted toward the front door of the store.

Moving fast, I threw the door open in one motion while scanning the store for the ice machine. Practically in a gallop now, I spotted the big white ice container with double doors. I quickly opened one door. There was no ice. I opened the other door. Gazing into this cavern of a box, I spotted a single, solitary bag of ice in the back left corner of the box. I reached in to grab it but it was too far back. I leaned further into the box, but I still could not even touch it. Next, I pushed my upper body, head, and left arm into the opening while holding onto the wet, cold, stainless steel side of the box with my right hand. Stretching with all my might to reach the bag, my foot slipped.

Instantly, I catapulted headfirst inside, face planted on the ice box bottom, and landed upside down on my back, floundering on the wet slippery floor of the ice box. I was astonished! The ice box ate me! I could not believe this was happening to me. Not only was my back wet and freezing cold, but I couldn't flip over onto my feet. It was as if the floor was coated with baby oil, and I was a turtle flipped over on its shell. I was wearing a T-shirt, swimsuit and flip-flops. Not exactly ice box attire.

I thought to myself, *How ridiculous. I have fallen into the ice box from hell.* Then I began to torture myself with wild thoughts. I could see the local headlines: "Man Freezes to Death While Family Waits Patiently in Parking Lot."

Think, Jack, think, I thought. *You have your cell phone. Maybe you could call 9-1-1 and tell them you are stuck in the ice cooler at the 7-Eleven. No, no, I I'll just yell for help.* All the while, I continued to spin around on my back like a turtle still unable to right itself. I thought to myself again, *How did this happen? What am I doing here?*

That's when I remembered I was here to buy a bag of ice. As long as I was stuck in that predicament, I was at least going to get that lone bag of ice. Sliding around the floor, I finally grabbed it.

Using the bag of ice and the excess water inside the bag, I was able to create a sort of plastic bubble and used it to roll over on my hands and knees. Holding onto the bag for stability, I grasped the bottom of the door opening, lifting the bag up and out of the cooler. Using my left hand, I grabbed the opening of the cooler and tried to stand up. My feet continued to slip and slide, hitting the back wall of the container. Finally, I stabilized myself. The door to freedom was only three feet away. Pushing off the back wall with my feet and legs while aiming my head and body at the opening of the box, I skied across the freezer and my head and upper body made it outside.

I felt like a seal at Sea World as I slithered out of the ice box onto the floor. As I lay there with my trophy bag of ice, I half-expected a trainer to throw me a sardine for my performance. Instead, I saw the manager looming over me.

"What in the world are you doing?" he said.

I told him the truth, that I needed some ice. He just walked away, shaking his head. I got off the floor and stood up, grabbed my bag of ice, and then realized I only had one flip-flop on. *Forget it.* Holding my head high and limping slightly, I made my way back outside to the truck.

Success Secret No. 21:

Look for the humor in every situation. Then figure out what you can learn from it.

Laughing at failures, mistakes, and unpredictable situations like my ice box experience lifts your spirits and those around you. It puts you in a better frame of mind to learn the lesson from the experience, unclouded by embarrassment, anger or frustration. Humor puts mistakes and messes into perspective and reminds you that, "This, too, shall pass."

Owning a business is a lot like the rest of life: Oddball and bizarre things will happen occasionally. You will fail. Mistakes will happen. Your response to these is key. Look for the humor and the lesson.

Admit it, forget it, and move forward.

Strike It Rich!

Success Secret No. 21: Look for the humor in every situation. Then figure out what you can learn from it.

Pure Veins of Gold

1. Listen to humorous podcasts, books, or radio on the way to work. If you are not naturally big on jokes and humor, develop your "funny bone" like you would any other skill.

2. Learn to tell a good, clean joke or two. Practice your delivery. See which jokes get you the best response.

3. Don't let a mistake or failure steal your joy. You can't grow without risk, and some risks will fail. Learn from them and move on. Don't get stuck down in the dumps, berating yourself for all the ways a deal went wrong. Move forward to the next one.

4. Remember that attitude trickles down from the top. If you are too serious, your staff will feel it and the tone in your office will be stern. Likewise, humor does not mean goofing off all the time. Strike a balance of fun and hard work and everyone will be more productive, innovative, and happier in their work.

Darth Vader Was Driving

*Success Secret No. 22: Never let your fear of failure
keep you from trying new things.*

*Success Secret No. 23: To win or be successful,
practice again and again. Visualize your steps to
success over and over. Then put them in motion.*

I could see "Big Daddy" Don Garlits in my side-view mirror
coming up fast. I couldn't believe it. I was racing one of the
greatest! I was spotted for seventeen car lengths, and I was racing
for real money. See, I had won bottom stock street eliminator N-
stock, and Don Garlits had won top eliminator. Now we were
neck and neck.

Only a minute ago I was sitting, nice and quiet at the burnout line,
scared to death and wondering, "How did I get here?" The
announcer on the public speaker system said, "Jack Arrington,
driving the black Olds, racing Don the 'Swamp Rat' Garlits."

How do they know my name? I thought. I was trembling all over.
Don pulled alongside me as close as he could and stood on the
gas. He was in neutral and the open pipes were shooting flames
along the side of my car. The noise was deafening. In my
inexperience and sheer panic, I forgot and left my window open. I
looked over once again. Daddy Don's car was a flame-breathing

monster with Darth Vader behind the wheel. He stepped on his accelerator again and smoke from his tires filled my car.

I was breathing racing fuel and smoke, coughing uncontrollably and rubbing my eyes as he was doing his burnout. The noise was earsplitting. He literally scared the piss out of me. I think he was trying to intimidate me. He succeeded. I stood on the gas to do my burnout. It putt-putted like an old sewing machine compared to Don's dragster. I pulled up beside Don at the starting line. I was so nervous I couldn't think. I was a kid racing a professional. I couldn't hear anything but the monster next to me. By now, I had closed my window. I hunched over the steering wheel, fully focused on the flag-wave start, but no one was there.

Suddenly, my concentration was shattered by someone pounding on the driver's side window. I opened it and the flagman leaned in, hollering in my ear, "See the man way out there with the flag? Go out there!" I was so nervous I forgot I had a seventeen car-length head start.

Fast-forward a few fleeting minutes, and now Don and I were nearly side by side. I pressed the accelerator, hoping he would break down. Nope. He flew by me at 180 miles an hour or more straight on to victory.

I lost that race to Big Daddy. Still, I knew I was a winner. How? Because I did something that was beyond my comfort level. I tried something new. I did not let the fear of failure stop me from trying.

Success Secret No. 22:

Never let your fear of failure keep you from trying new things.

Let me explain how I got to that racetrack on that memorable night. It was during the time I worked at Publix, and my friends and I were obsessed with muscle cars. They were the hot new cars to have. For new car dealers, the popular slogan of the day was, "Win on Sunday. Sell on Monday." This was a pure vein of gold for salesmen. They would drive up to the grocery store in these muscle cars, hand out brochures, take us to lunch, and let us drive them.

We had good jobs and most of us had some savings from our tip money that could be used for a down payment. My friend Bob Locht bought a 1963 Dodge 383 with floor shifter. My other friend bought a 409 Chevrolet. On Sundays I would go to the drag strip and watch them race. They wanted me to race my old 1949 Oldsmobile straight-8 and would not take no for an answer. Not being one to back away from a challenge, I raced and won against four other cars in my class. I could hardly believe it. Kathy was very excited each time I came back to the pits. She would jump up and down, showering me with kisses.

Having completed the lower brackets and won each race, I qualified for bottom stock eliminator and the opportunity to continue to race. I won two more times. My good friends Nick Damato and Paul Celli, along with Bob and Kathy, could not believe what I did. I felt ecstatic. I got the "racing bug" that day.

I took the car to Bert Smith Oldsmobile dealership for a tune-up to be ready for the race on the following weekend. The service representative asked me what was wrong with the car. I explained that I wanted it tuned so it would go as fast as it possibly could. I told him I was running it at the drag races. The representative told me the best man for the job was Clyde Walters, an older man who really knew older cars. Clyde and I clicked immediately. He also had raced and enjoyed my story of winning the races the previous Sunday.

"I will tune up the old girl and service everything," Clyde said, "and I would like to accompany you to the track on Sunday and help you win."

Wow! My own pit crew, I thought to myself. Clyde told me to drop my car off on Saturday morning and he would spend the day getting it ready.

"Clyde, you and I both know this is a stock car only," I said.

"I know, however, I am an expert and I will keep the car legal," Clyde replied.

"What are you going to do?" I asked nervously.

"I am going to unlock the back brakes," Clyde said. "This will help you get off the line quicker. Most likely, your automatic transmission is shifting four times before you get to the quarter-mile. I will adjust it to shift only three times, and you may be able to pick up a whole second."

I was uncertain about the brakes, as it sounded dangerous to me. Clyde reassuringly said, "You've got to trust me. I will fix the brakes back after the race."

My mind conjured up visions of me and my pit crew on our way to the Indianapolis 500. The next morning, Nick and I picked up Kathy, the car, and my crew chief Clyde, who followed behind us in his big box truck filled with an entire automotive shop inside.

All my friends came out that day. I was the center of attention. I went out for my first practice run. I could tell I was much faster. I read the time: 16.8. I did not know it at the time, but I tied the best mark in the nation for N-stock that year. Over the next four weeks, I got faster and faster. With each win, we worked our way up to the money run with Big Daddy Don Garlits.

Clyde was indeed an expert at getting the car and me to perform to the maximum. He showed me how to sit in a chair and visualize the quick start off the line. I must have done it a thousand times. I was ready. After every run he pulled each spark plug and cleaned them. He checked the air pressure in all four tires. Remember this: In business and in life, it is the details repeated over and over again that allow you to be successful.

Success Secret No. 23:

To win or be successful, practice again and again. Visualize your steps to success over and over. Then put them in motion. The instruction manual for mankind says that as a man thinks in his heart, so is he.[7] See yourself winning.

After "Darth Vader" Garlits defeated me, I raced five more weeks but never made it back to the money runs. I sold my car, took all my savings, and bought the Corvette. I will always remember the first time I picked up Kathy in the Corvette. She was ecstatic and loved it. Her parents could not believe I was driving such an expensive, showy sports car.

Don Garlits remained in drag racing and went on to become known as the Father of Drag Racing, eventually opening his personal museum to the public in Ocala, Fla.[8] If you love racing, this is a must-see experience. You can even see the car that beat me: Swamp Rat II.

Even if you grew up being called a failure, as I did, you can achieve great things if you keep trying new things. I tried working in lawn maintenance. That later led to my owning lawn maintenance companies. I tried working at a restaurant. That gave me the skills to deal with people and to move quickly and efficiently. I tried working for a grocery store and learned invaluable lessons from my customers such as how to invest in the stock market. I also learned the power of tips and compound interest. I tried acquiring real estate and ended up with tenants who paid my mortgage.

Do you think I was scared to try these new things? Absolutely. Every time. But I also knew that to grow I had to dive into the deep end and figure out how to kick and paddle until I could swim.

David Van Rooy, the senior director of Global Leadership Development at Walmart, put it like this in his book *Trajectory: 7 Career Strategies To Take You From Where You Are To Where You Want To Be:*

> "I've seen in my work at Walmart that maintaining placement as the top retailer requires staying ahead of change and a willingness to 'swim upstream.' So much of what everyone does at Walmart – whether it is the size or scale of an endeavor, or launching an entirely new idea – has never been done before. This can be daunting because it includes an element of risk and necessitates people stepping out of their comfort zones. The people who do this successfully are able to make a tremendously positive impact and find even more opportunities to make a difference. This can create a fast track for accelerating their career trajectory. It is possible to be successful maintaining the status quo, but true differentiation is achievable only for those who are willing to dive into new areas." [9]

My success is proof that no matter what your childhood looked like, no matter how much education you lack, you can succeed. It takes hard work and the determination to be different, but you can do it. You might not beat Darth Vader, but you'll still be a winner when you cross that finish line!

Strike It Rich!

Success Secret No. 22: Never let your fear of failure keep you from trying new things.

Success Secret No. 23: To win or be successful, practice again and again. Visualize your steps to success over and over. Then put them in motion.

Pure Veins of Gold

1. What have you been putting off because it feels too hard? Write it down. Look at it on the paper. What do you need to get it done? Education? Find someone to help you. Time? Put it on your calendar and stick to it. Encouragement? Find someone to hold you accountable and cheer you on. Accomplishing something you've been procrastinating about is a major milestone to success.

2. Take a few minutes at the beginning and end of your day to visualize something you want to change or achieve in your life. Want to write a novel? Picture yourself typing the pages, all the way to the final "The End." Want to learn Chinese? Picture yourself in China, speaking to natives as you see the sights. Visualize what you are going to do and how you are going to do it. Then get started!

3. If at first you don't succeed ... you know the rest. Keep trying. Don't give up. I didn't learn to read until I was in my thirties. Yes, my thirties! It took years of dedication, determination, and practice, practice, practice. If you have a passion, pursue it and practice it.

Well, You Do the Math!

Success Secret No. 24: Don't be afraid to make the right paradigm shifts in your attitude, outlook, and company. Sometimes you need to change your business model to grow your company. Sometimes you need to change your thinking to grow yourself.

There was a three-year period shortly after we got started when both of our businesses grew quickly. We had about twenty employees when Arrington Grounds Maintenance changed its business model from mowing and landscaping private homes to servicing only commercial properties. The difference was that where we had been netting six thousand dollars per month for individual homes, the change equated to more than sixty thousand dollars per month for large condominium and industrial complexes.

Well, you do the math!

Success Secret No. 24:

Don't be afraid to make the right paradigm shifts in your attitude, outlook, and company. Sometimes you need to change your business model to grow your company.

We secured written agreements with major companies in the Tampa Bay area like United States Steel, Honeywell, Allstate, Raymond James, Jim Walters, GTE, SunTrust Banks, Bank of America, and the *Tampa Bay Times*, just to name a few.

Our company's reputation was excellent. We showed when we promised. We were on time. We always did our best. This operational philosophy caused potential new customers to seek us out, rather than my having to go out and sell all the time. All the details of a job, repeated well, are the secret to success.

I was a talented salesman both in person and over a telephone. At first, I was always in so much of a hurry that the importance of dressing properly and professionally for business meetings wasn't at the top of my priority list. This changed quickly. One time, I went to a new bank to secure a low-interest loan for the purchase of a dump truck. It had been my experience that it is best always to speak directly to the head person at the bank, bypassing the loan department. Carrying all the necessary paperwork with me, I walked into the bank in dirty, sweaty work clothes and mud-clogged boots after a long day of landscaping. I smelled a bit rank. Needless to say, I did not look like the owner of a multimillion-dollar business.

The bank lady asked me how much I made each year and I told her. She looked me straight in the eyes and said, "No, that amount is what your company makes in a year. That is called your gross income for the year."

"No, that is how much I made," I returned.

"No, Mr. Arrington, you could not have made that much," she insisted. "I am sure you are confusing that number with your gross." Her voice was now stern, while still maintaining politeness.

I was getting a little irritated with her at this point. "How much do you make a year?" I asked.

"Well, I can't tell you that," she replied.

"If you could tell me what you made, that figure would be your net income, right?" I asked. "See, you are not asking me the right question."

"Okay, Mr. Arrington, how much money do you gross a year?" she said.

"Ten times more than I net!" I replied.

This time, she finally got it. When I showed her my tax return from the previous year, her face went ashen. Needless to say, I received the truck loan and saved 1.25 percent on the interest.

***

During this rapid-growth phase, I found it hard to keep up with the learning curve. I needed help managing all the people, schedules and the diversity of my companies. I found myself getting depressed. During these times, my cheerleader Kathy would give me the " Two bits, Four bits" cheer. This always made me laugh, and she would assure me I could do it. "I know you can," she would sweetly say with that gorgeous smile and twinkling eyes. I had her permission to win.

During this growth period, I also proved to be very competent at borrowing money. In hardly any time at all, I found myself with more than one million dollars in debt. To suggest that I was a bit freaked out is a fair statement, or even an understatement. About this time I listened to a radio interview by a man named Charlie Haslam. He owned the largest bookstore in the southeastern United States. He had read more than five thousand books and had six million new and used books for sale. He had also traveled to every free country in the world. The interview was about how to operate a business. *This man must be smart,* I thought. *He owns Haslam's Book Store in St. Petersburg, Florida. Plus, he is right here in my own city.*

Once again I remembered Dad telling me, "Ask and you will receive." I drove downtown to Haslam's, determined to find and meet this man. When I got there, I was told that Mr. Haslam was in Africa. No one was certain of his return date. My disappointment was equal to a balloon that has lost its air. I felt completely deflated. I asked them to call me when he came back to town. Deep in my spirit, I knew he could help me. Over the course of the next several weeks, I stopped in at the bookstore on more than one occasion to see if the gallivanting Mr. Haslam had returned. Each time, I left my name and phone number in the hope that he would call.

One day, he did.

I shared with Mr. Haslam that I had listened to his radio interview on how to succeed in business and from that very moment knew I must speak to him in person. We made an appointment for the following week. I arrived half an hour early. Remember: It is better to be an hour early than a minute late.

I told one of the store clerks that I had a one o'clock meeting with Mr. Haslam. She offered me a chair close to his office door. He came out immediately and gave me a warm welcome while exclaiming, "At least one person was listening to what I had to say."

"The interview was fascinating and I am so pleased to get to meet you," I said.

"Well, Jack, come on into my office and if you can find a chair, sit down," Mr. Haslam said. His office can best be described as a cave of old books, piled to the ceiling. There were stacks and stacks of books falling on top of each other. I made my way through the maze of stacks and found one chair unoccupied by books.

Mr. Haslam said he had half an hour and asked me to come directly to the point. "What do you want?" he asked.

"I want to be rich," I replied.

"What kind of rich do you want to be?" he said.

"Money rich," I said, thinking it an odd question.

"I can teach you how to make money, but first I need to tell you about Jesus," Mr. Haslam replied in his kindly, country-Southern drawl. It was the kind of drawl that turns a one-syllable word into two syllables and a two-syllable word into at least three or four. His delivery of the name "Jesus" sounded something like *Jeez-zus*, with the accent on the *Jeez*.

I told him that I did not want to know about Jesus. I wanted to be rich. He told me that he would not tell me how to get rich unless he could tell me about Jeez-zus. "Okay, let's hear it," I finally said.

Mr. Haslam started out by telling me that first I needed to experience a paradigm shift in my thinking and attitude. I asked what a paradigm was. He told me that a paradigm shift in one's thinking is a fundamental change in one's underlying assumptions.

"Jack," he said, "this is very simple." He picked up an old, well-worn Bible from his desk and began explaining a scripture verse.

> John 10:10b (NASB): "I came that they may have life and have it abundantly."

"Do you want life and a life more abundantly, Jack?" Mr. Haslam asked me directly.

"Yes!" I replied enthusiastically.

He then told me about the devil who comes only to steal, kill, and destroy.

"What do you think, Jack?" He asked after he stated his beliefs.

"I do not believe in Jesus, and I definitely don't believe in a devil," I said.

Mr. Haslam began asking me questions, starting with, "Do you ever write down the date?"

"Of course I do," I responded.

"Our entire calendar system and time is based on Jesus's birth. He is the Alpha and Omega, the beginning and the end," Mr. Haslam said. "Do you celebrate Christmas and Easter?"

"Yes, I do," I answered.

"Those events are based on Jesus's birth, life, death, and resurrection," he said.

Then, without so much as a blink of an eye or taking in of breath, he changed the subject. He began questioning me about business. What business was I in? How did I get started? How long had I been in business? Did I have goals for my business?

When I answered, he was either shocked or impressed with how much debt I had acquired, as his eyes opened wide like saucers. Then he wanted to know about my education, where I went to college, etc. I told him that I attended the university of "right now."

Mr. Haslam did not say a word about my lack of education. Instead, looking at his watch, he said, "You need to read the following books. They are business classics: *The Power of Positive Thinking* by Norman Vincent Peale, *Acres of Diamonds* by Russell Conwell, *Think and Grow Rich* by Napoleon Hill and, most important of all, the Bible.

"It is called the Good News, and it is an instruction manual for mankind," he said. "First, read the book of Proverbs and then Psalms. Jack, if you get nothing else from our discussion today, at least remember this: Knowing the right books to read and learning about the men who wrote them are essentials to success. Study their lives, as that will help you understand their books. Having the right knowledge and an enthusiastic attitude will make you rich in every area of your life – body, soul and spirit."

Mr. Haslam explained that reading one classic self-help book that he recommended would be the equivalent of reading ten substandard books on the same subject. At this point, the wheels of the knowledge train almost fell off the track when I confessed to Mr. Haslam that I could not read. This time there was no mistaking the look on his face. It was pure shock.

"Jack, don't you know you are sitting in the largest book store in the southeast?" He said. "You must be able to read if I am to help you."

"I have thought about paying one of my wife's friends who needs a job to record the books," I said. "I can listen to them in my truck and on the job."

"That is a great idea, Jack, but you still must learn how to read," he said

My precious wife had worked with me on and off through the years since I got kicked out of school to help me learn. But I had difficulty catching on. I am sure today I would be quickly diagnosed with dyslexia or another learning disability and perhaps given the tools I needed to succeed and learn in school. Instead, I was just labeled "stupid" and shown the door. My book learning had reached a standstill. Now I was determined to throw the door wide open.

The encouragement from Mr. Haslam, followed by my dedication to absorb learning by listening to books on tape, opened up all new streams of understanding and wisdom. Over the course of the rest of that year, Mr. Haslam met with me about six times. Each time, he talked first about Jesus. He explained that I should be concerned with becoming rich in every area of my life: body, soul and spirit. He reiterated that Jesus Christ came so that I might have life and life more abundantly. As the days went by, I listened to each tape at least a hundred times. Mr. Haslam selected more and more books for me to listen to on business and self-improvement.

One time, Mr. Haslam told me about Merriam Webster and his original dictionary. Mr. Haslam was in possession of an old one, which he gave to me. He wanted me to have an edition that was not changed to apply "liberal meanings" to words. I didn't have a clue what he was talking about. Then he showed me the word "enthusiasm."

He looked at me intently. "Jack, you have enthusiasm, and enthusiasm means to be inspired by God with special revelation from the Holy Spirit of God," he said.

I could hardly believe what he just said. *I am inspired by God, with special revelation from the Holy Spirit? Wow, what a thought! God is for me.*

At this time in my life, my sons were still in elementary school. My son Tim was learning to read, and I paid the reading teacher to meet with me in the evenings to practice my own reading skills. Over time, I painstakingly learned to read and write. I was still a slow reader and could absorb information much more quickly by listening to it, but I finally did learn to read.

Meeting with Mr. Haslam gave me a successful mentor to look up to, and his wisdom was invaluable in my life. He spurred a paradigm shift in my thinking, and I realigned my priorities and my definition of success. This shift in my beliefs, attitudes, and even business model gave me true success in every area of my life.

Strike It Rich!

Success Secret No. 24: Don't be afraid to make the right paradigm shifts in your attitude, outlook, and company. Sometimes you need to change your business model to grow your company.

Pure Veins of Gold

1. Always negotiate everything with the bank manager who makes the decisions. Banks may have its standards, but you should also have your standard that the bank should meet.

2. Always dress appropriately when working with office professionals, particularly on the financial side of your business. When you want to borrow money, look like someone who makes money and is a worthy investment.

3. If anyone you respect uses a phrase similar to this one: "If you get nothing else from our discussion today, at least remember this …" perk up and listen. It will be a pure vein of gold.

4. When you own your own service business, there will be times when it is necessary to seek professional assistance and advice to help you earn and keep money. Do your homework on any advisors before you take their advice. If you want to learn more about sales, make appointments with top salespeople. Learn from long-timers who have plenty of experience. Find out what paved the way to their biggest successes and what pitfalls led to their biggest failures. Be careful and cautious before partnering with others.

Smooth-Talking Stranger In
A Silk Suit

Success Secret No. 25: Possessing the Holy Spirit in your life allows you to be tapped into the wisdom of the God of the universe.

Success Secret No. 26: A problem defined is half-solved.

During our mentoring year, Mr. Haslam taught me how to think more accurately and to look for opportunities to learn from the best of the best. I followed this advice and learned of a man named Sir Lionel Luckhoo, the only person to be the ambassador for two countries at the same time. Due to his work as an attorney, he is listed in the *Guinness Book of World Records* for winning 245 consecutive defense cases.

One time, Sir Luckhoo was to speak at a business luncheon in St. Petersburg, so I made a point of arriving early to get a front row seat. (Tip: Sitting in front gives you the opportunity to see a speaker's facial expressions and body language.) His clothing was exquisite. He wore a custom dark silk suit and a white dress shirt with French cuffs sporting gold cuff links. A silk scarf peeked out of his chest pocket. He looked very impressive.

After greeting everyone, Sir Luckhoo began with a story of a boy who wanted to be the smartest person in the world and set out to do just that. This boy spent all of his time learning and learning, more and more. The boy set goals for himself. I could tell this man was extremely intelligent, and my fascination with his prelude deepened as he continued to speak. He told how the boy grew and as he did, he learned that there were three major things that would allow him to achieve. Luckhoo said the three things were the following: people, preparation, and process. As he grew, the young man attended one of the finest colleges in the world. He purposed to be the valedictorian, to learn as much as he could.

Of course, it soon became apparent that Sir Lionel Luckhoo was referring to himself.

As time passed, Sir Luckhoo acquired two trunks filled with diplomas, degrees, certificates of completion, and awards on just about every subject imaginable. By the age of sixty-four, he had accomplished all of his goals, achieved an extremely elevated status in society, and was admired by colleagues and contemporaries. Queen Elizabeth II knighted him. His wealth was so great that he owned more than one hundred racehorses. He was success personified.

Unfortunately, even with knowledge, prestige, and wealth, happiness and contentment were nowhere to be found, Sir Luckhoo told the crowd. He had trouble sleeping. As the months went by, he couldn't figure out what was wrong, even with all his vast scholastic knowledge and experience. About this time, he was invited to attend a Full Gospel business fellowship meeting in Chattanooga, Tennessee, where he heard about a person named Jesus the Christ.

That very night, Sir Luckhoo expressed his faith in Jesus, asking for forgiveness of his sins and committed his life to Him. He became a changed man. Peacefulness and restful sleep came immediately to him. He then shared how Jesus's love is for everyone and what an incredible difference his personal relationship with God made in giving real meaning to his life. For me, this became another pure vein of gold.

Success Secret No. 25:

Possessing the Holy Spirit in your life allows you to be tapped into the wisdom of the God of the universe.

After the meeting, I had the opportunity to meet Sir Luckhoo. I asked him if he had the time to meet with me to discuss business. He said he would if I could accompany him around the city the next day. He was to speak at the Stetson University College of Law, where he was presenting the trial of Jesus Christ. I had the privilege of spending most of the day with him. During that time I asked him point-blank, "What do you consider to be the secret of your success?"

"I have learned to look at business, law, thinking, and studying through the lens of three filters or categories: people, preparation and process," Luckhoo said. "However, all three are also all-in-one."

"What do you mean?" I asked.

"Let me explain," Sir Luckhoo said. "The Bible talks about the Father, Son, and Holy Spirit as one."

"How can this be?" I said.

"Take a block of ice and place it in the sun," Sir Luckhoo said. "It turns to water and then to vapor and disappears. You see, it is three parts but yet all in one. Every law case was about people, preparation, and process. That is how I won my cases. I prepared three different detailed strategies for a particular trial and kept them in my briefcase ready for use. I could then change my strategy instantly if I needed to.

"Remember, you might only have one opportunity in front of the judge, or, in the case of business, in front of the decision maker of a company. Therefore, you must make that opportunity count."

I took this advice and applied it to selling landscape maintenance contracts to Fortune 500 companies. Every time I was with the decision maker of the company, I was ready. I always prepared three ways to acquire their business. I began to win five out of every seven sales attempts. This success rate was unheard of at the time.

The depth of preparation and the information I studied about the company itself aided the decision maker in making the right decision – me. I prepared a form for companies I solicited, listing six difficult questions they should ask the competition. I researched each company and prepared the answers, offering pictures and video as well. Because I had all the answers, it quickly became obvious that my company was the best choice. It all came back to people, preparation, and process. I have much to thank Sir Lionel Luckhoo for.

***

From these last chapters, I hope you see how important it is for entrepreneurs to have other businessmen they trust and respect to learn from and even partner with. Among a select group of businessmen I most admire is a gentleman named Tom Chapman. When Tom was only twenty-seven years old, he led the entire nation of more than six thousand Massachusetts Life Insurance Company agents in sales. These types of insurance policies often produce residual income throughout the life of the policy. It is a smart business practice to create income that duplicates itself without having to do additional work.

Tom has been my friend and mentor for the past thirty years. He started and built Advanced Protection Technologies, a company which produces and sells surge protection equipment worldwide. His company employs 125 people. Simultaneously, he bought orange groves in Florida for development purposes. Recently, he purchased a fifteen-hundred-acre track, perhaps the largest parcel available, near the Orlando area. It is extremely valuable now. In the future it will be much more so. From Tom I have learned the importance of preparation, perseverance, and consistency.

Tom is not only an important businessman, but also he is truly God's man. He conducts his businesses in accordance with biblical wisdom and principles. One of the top men at Advanced Protection Technologies (APT) was Ed Harrold, who was hired to build the company's management information system. Tom was able to woo Ed away from Honeywell where Ed helped lead his team in the development of the U.S. military's GPS system. This is the directional system that we all use and take for granted today.

One time, Tom told me that Ed was going to offer a series of lectures teaching from a book titled *Wild at Heart* by an author named John Eldredge. The sessions would be held as early as six o'clock in the morning in Ed's office prior to everyone's work day beginning. He asked me if I would be interested in attending. If you are invited by your mentor to attend a meeting where solid teaching is presented, don't think twice. Do it! I said yes.

On time and ready to learn, I arrived to find nine other men, all of whom had attended college and received their engineering degrees. Over the next three months, I learned from Ed the secret of a man's soul. According to Eldredge, deep in his heart every man longs for a battle to fight, an adventure to live, and a beauty to rescue.

Ed told us that Eldredge says men should not ask themselves, "What does the world need from me?" but rather, "What makes me come alive?" The world needs men who have come alive. Ed and I became very close friends over time. He was fascinated by my common sense and life experiences and often asked me open-ended questions.

Later, Ed left APT to pursue his dream of building his own business, and he and I founded a company called Wise Apps, LLC. Apps were the wave of the future, and Ed and I both knew that a problem defined is half-solved. If we could define the problems, the missing elements for companies and customers alike, we could create apps that filled the gaps and fit the needs. We'd be golden.

Success Secret No. 26:

A problem defined is half-solved.

This was at the very beginning of cell phone applications and downloads. Our plan was for Ed to design and develop apps, and I would handle the marketing and sales. Our goal was to create apps that would produce monthly cash flow. Ed is an incredibly humble and unassuming man, a father of seven kids, and not one to talk himself up. However, over time I came to realize how brilliant Ed is. I learned that he was an online professor at Regent University where he taught app development and computer science. Even more impressive was the fact that the Massachusetts Institute of Technology (MIT) called on Ed as a consultant to help solve their computer problems. He even had a black belt in karate.

It took me nine months of asking if he was a genius to find out that his IQ score placed him in the top one-fourth percent of genius-level people in the world. I was in business with an intellectual superstar.

One day, I met Ed at his home to work. The Harrolds' Florida home was in a lovely, riverfront setting surrounded by several acres of woods and swamp. I could tell that Ed was just not himself so I asked him if he was all right. He told me that his wife Jane was very upset with him for not supervising their youngest daughter and her friend properly while Jane went shopping. She was gone for approximately four hours while he was working on the development of an app that required using three computer screens at the same time. He became so focused that he forgot to watch the children.

When Jane returned home, she heard their dog Rusty barking frantically while running circles around the girls, who were playing on the fishing dock by the river. Running toward the girls, Jane saw a large animal near them shaped like an alligator. In full-blown panic mode and yelling for Ed at the top of her lungs, Jane fully saw the monster. It was a huge ten-foot gator, and to Jane's horror, the girls were jumping on him!

As Jane approached, she saw that the alligator was dead and lying on its back. The girls were laughing and screaming as they jumped on its bloated stomach, making the alligator pass gas. (What a hoot to listen to the toot!) It baffled everyone as to how the youngsters were able to pull that big, heavy alligator out of the water and onto the dock. Poor Ed. He wasn't trusted to watch the children for a long time after that, but boy did we have a good story!

Okay, back to business. As Ed developed the apps, I quickly sold five of them. One was designed for a drug rehabilitation clinic in South America. Every app Ed developed was so perfect that they all sold immediately. We had been in business less than a year when Ed's work captured the attention of Google. Google was so impressed with Ed's results that they invited him to participate in a contest designed to solve an extremely complex problem. More than one hundred thousand participants entered the contest. Ed not only solved the problem, but he accomplished it so quickly that Google was astounded and called with a job offer too wonderful to pass up. Our company dissolved and Ed moved ahead with Google.

My business belief had always been, "Don't strive for perfection; strive for results." Ed taught me to strive for perfection too, and excellent results will follow.

Strike It Rich!

Success Secret No. 25: Possessing the Holy Spirit in one's life allows one to be tapped into the wisdom of the God of the universe.

Success Secret No. 26: A problem defined is half-solved.

Pure Veins of Gold

1. If you have never considered reading the Bible or making a belief in Christ a priority in your life, one of the best pieces of advices I can give you is to start reading and start following Him now. He is not a God of rules and regulations who is out to get you for what you do wrong or keep you from having the fun you want to have. He is come to give you life, and life more abundantly (Read John 10:10). He also promises to give you "a future and a hope." (Jeremiah 29:11). If you read the top business books and self-improvement books and then read the book of Proverbs and the New Testament in the Bible, you will find that almost all of the "best practices" in business are based on principles written in God's instruction manual thousands of years ago. They still apply in a fresh way today. Give it a shot. What have you got to lose?

2. Find business mentors willing to invest time in you. Soak up their knowledge, wisdom, and experience like a sponge.

3. Hang around and partner with people with different skillsets and different ways of thinking and solving problems than you have. Ed and I are very different in

the way we think and operate. When we put our strengths together, the sum was more than its parts.

4. Look at the companies and customers around you. What are they missing? What do they need to run more efficiently or make their lives easier? Ask your current customers. If you can find a "missing piece" for a company or fill gaps for your customers, you have defined a problem and you are already halfway there to solving it. When you can do that, you've hit a pure vein of gold!

5. If you ever want to hear something funny, jump on the belly of a big dead bull alligator!

Laughing Grass

Success Secret No. 27: Practice preparation, perseverance, and consistency.

I want to tell you about my biggest achievement. Although I hope I have given you plenty of tips to help you run a profitable service business and, even better, your own life in many ways, my biggest success stories are not my multimillion-dollar companies, my positions on boards, my awards or accolades. No, by far my greatest success is love, the enduring love of Christ and the love I have for my wife Kathy and our two sons. All the money and success in the world could not replace it.

From my son Kenny, I learned that tomorrow is never guaranteed. There is only this moment, the present. It is called the present because it is a gift to you. Use it wisely.

From Tim I learned that great joy can be found in working with someone you love. Let me tell you about my older son Tim, with whom I am well pleased. Tim used to work as a Special Weapons And Tactics (SWAT) officer for a local city police department. He was such a good shot that he could hit a penny with a rifle from one hundred yards. He is a strong "man's man." All his life, his unusual and extraordinary sense of humor kept everyone around him laughing and in a good mood. Many of his friends consider him a gifted amateur comedian.

One day Tim came to me and announced his intention to marry. "Dad, I know Christy is the one," he said. "I'm going to ask her to marry me." He then told me that even though he enjoyed law enforcement, he couldn't see continuing that career because it is very stressful on marriages. With this in mind, he and I devised a plan for a new service business.

Right off the bat, I knew this was going to be fun. We were already in the commercial lawn service business and the sprinkler systems maintenance business. Tim decided he would start a yard fertilizing, insect and weed control business, with expansion plans for an indoor pest control business. He had all kinds of creative, fun ideas on how to market and advertise a start-up business. One of the most important aspects of starting a business is selecting the name of the company. After three months of deliberating, he decided on the name Laughing Grass.

Over a period of five years, Tim built the Laughing Grass Company to more than one thousand customer agreements. In my opinion, he made seven key creative moves that started him off with success. I'll let you in on his secrets:

1. He came up with an excellent name that gained positive attention.

2. He created a cartoon logo to help brand his company. The artwork on the company trucks featured animated blades of grass that were laughing and happy. They were eye-catching, cute, and creative.

3. He installed a sound system in the company trucks with outside speakers so that every time the truck stopped, people would hear the truck laughing. (Genius!)

4. He branded the cartoon logos on all written materials.

5. He branded the company shirts and hats with his logo.

6. He set company goals for acquiring customer agreements.

7. He studied and received his state license, quickly becoming an expert in fertilizers and insect control.

During the five years Tim spent growing the Laughing Grass organization, he also invested in real estate. This became a moneymaker and provided Tim the opportunity to learn and become proficient at another set of transferable skills.

Success Secret No. 27:

Practice preparation, perseverance, and consistency.

In this short five-year period, the Laughing Grass Company became so successful that there was greater value in selling it than operating it. We sold it to a national company who made us an offer we could not refuse. The company purchased the entire service business – all the agreements, equipment, and vehicles.

We have done it and so can you. You have only one life – one opportunity to grow, learn, strive, fail, get back up, love, build, and create. You have one life to live, one finite amount of time to spend. What legacy will you leave? Who will you serve? How much love will you pass on? How will you be remembered? What will you make?

Remember to make more love than you make money. Love leaves a legacy money can't buy. Whatever you do, do it to the very best of your ability.

Don't let anybody tell you you're not capable. You are. You are the only you this world has ever known. You were created to create your very own best life.

Strike It Rich!

Success Secret No. 27: Practice preparation, perseverance, and consistency. Make the most of every day!

Pure Veins of Gold

1. Customer relationships and customer agreements are the most valuable assets of a service company.

2. Do things you can duplicate.

3. Generating continuous cash flow is the key to the growth of a service business. Sell, sell, sell. Everyone in your company should be able to sell. If they don't know how, teach them.

4. Hire sales representatives as independent contractors and pay them commission from the sales they generate. Commission-only sales that are based on new sales, new money, alleviate hiring a person "on staff." A person in a company staff position causes additional and often expensive paper records and Department of Labor requirements to be maintained, while a subcontractor status does not. Contact your accountant and local authorities to determine the laws that apply to subcontractors vs. employees.

5. Make more love than you make money. Love leaves a legacy money can't buy.

Closing Thoughts

People frequently use the axiom and songs are written proclaiming that there is always tomorrow. This is not true. At the age of twenty, our youngest son Kenny died in a fall down a flight of steps. He was gone in an instant.

The day before the accident as we said goodbye, Kenny said to us, "I love you, Mom and Dad." My wife and I hugged him and told him that we loved him too.

Those were our last words to each other. We treasure those words and hold them close to our hearts until the joy of seeing him again.

Remember:

There is no guarantee of tomorrow, only today.

Make it a masterpiece.

Afterword by Kathy Arrington, Jack's Bride of Fifty-One Beautiful Years

Dear Readers,

I hope you caught a glimpse of just how special, determined, and truly smart Jack Arrington was. Even more, I hope you were inspired by his words and learned some wisdom you can take away and apply in your own lives and businesses.

True success is not determined by how you start the race of life, rather by how you finish. You can start life *Without a Dime* and finish with immeasurable riches. The riches that matter are the deposits and treasures you leave behind in the hearts and lives of those you loved and helped throughout your years.

In the following pages, I am blessed to share with you how the principles Jack wrote in this book are truth when put into action. The evidence is witnessed in the words of our two grandsons, Corey and Casey Arrington, who share in the following pages their love and the impact their grandfather had in their lives and that they will carry into future generations.

These are the eulogies Corey and Casey delivered in honor of my husband and best friend, Jack Arrington, at his memorial service:

Tribute from Corey Arrington:

Many of you know who I am. For those who do not, I am Corey Arrington, Jack's middle grandchild and the son of Tim. I just wanted to thank everyone in this room and everyone who wanted to be here on behalf of my family for the love and support you provided us over the last few weeks. Grandpa's only concern at the end was making sure his family would be taken care of, and you have done a better job than any of us could have ever imagined at making sure we are going to be okay.

After spending a few days with my grandpa at Hospice and now standing here today, I have finally been able to see the inspirational and positive impact he had on so many different people of all ages. God calls us to be a servant of His on this Earth, and it is comforting to see how well Grandpa excelled at serving his Lord and Savior. Grandpa truly was a man who strived to make those around him better; this is, in my opinion, one of his most respectable achievements and I couldn't be more proud of him for that.

Just over a year ago, Grandpa tried his hardest to have me speak at his 50th wedding anniversary. He told me it was better to speak about him while he was alive and listening than when he was no longer around to hear me. I did not speak at the anniversary, mostly because I assumed I would have another opportunity. Little did I know the next opportunity I would have to speak about Grandpa would be here today. Thankfully, I have a certain peace about me because someone showed me Hebrews 12:1 (NIV), which states, "Therefore, since we are surrounded by such a great cloud of witnesses, let us throw off everything that hinders and the sin that so easily entangles." I believe that Grandpa is in that cloud of witnesses. Therefore, he will be able to hear what I have to say. One time Grandpa told me I'd better not be a crying mess when he was taken home. He said to celebrate his life, so that is what we are going to do today.

In my junior year of high school, I was given the privilege to give a speech about my true American hero. I was told to choose someone who inspires others as well as myself to live our lives in a different, more positive way. After about three seconds of thought, I knew I would tell the class about my grandpa, who was the most positive influence in my life. A few nights before my speech, I called him and told him that he is my American hero and I would be telling my class his story, as well as my reasons for choosing him as my hero. Grandpa was at a loss for words because it was such an honor to him to be his grandson's hero. I was able to interview Grandpa and ask him questions about his childhood, meeting my grandma, his young adulthood, how he became saved, and who inspired him during his life. Today, I will be sharing most of that speech with you all to fill in those who do not know about his childhood as well as to celebrate his distinguished life.

An inspiration is someone who beats the odds to become something spectacular in life, and my grandpa is the best example of an inspiration. He was born October 27, 1943, in Ashland, Kentucky, where he lived for the next 11 years before moving to St. Petersburg. I asked Grandpa about the people he learned from as a child and the first person he mentioned was his Uncle Hagar. Hagar was a member of the Black Devils in World War II, which were the first army rangers. He taught my grandpa about respect and life in general. Grandpa's father Arnold taught him countless lessons about common sense, despite his second grade education. His first interactions with God came with the help of his Uncle Stanley, who introduced him to the Lord's Prayer. All three of these men had a lasting impact on Grandpa's life, and he always talked so proudly of them.

When Grandpa was in school, he wasn't necessarily a star student or on the honor roll. He enjoyed goofing off, skipping, not doing his work, and spending a lot of time with the principal. One time Grandpa and one of his buddies were sent to get spankings and his friend went first. His friend's head was against the wall when the principal unloaded on his posterior. He was spanked so hard that his head smashed against the wall, knocking him unconscious. Luckily for Grandpa, he got out of spankings that day.

After going to nine different schools in St. Petersburg, he was finally kicked out of school at the age of sixteen. Grandpa told me the people from the school system said he was an idiot, wouldn't make it anywhere in life, and his only slim hope was to become a mechanic. Grandpa wasn't necessarily a handy man but he was able to get a job as a bag boy at Publix. He got paid minimum wage but hustled his butt off to make as many tips as possible carrying groceries to cars. He worked so hard for tips that he was able to buy two Corvettes in his time there.

Grandpa worked at Publix for a long time and had a pretty simple life with his wife and two kids but said he felt something was missing. He used to do pull-ups on the door of the Publix bathroom to stay in shape, and he would always do them outside of the bathroom facing in. One day he decided to do them from inside the bathroom facing the hallway. Now, right inside the bathroom was a light bulb just above the door, so on his first pull-up his head crushed the light bulb and it exploded as Grandpa hit the floor. The bathroom became pitch black and he told me he truly thought he had died. When he realized he was still living, he told himself he needed to strive for something better in life than Publix.

So at age thirty he went to a bookstore in St. Petersburg and talked to a man named Mr. Haslam. Mr. Haslam had read over five thousand books and had six million in his store. My grandpa came to him and told him he wanted to become rich. Mr. Haslam said he wouldn't teach him anything unless he could share Jesus with him for twenty minutes. Grandpa agreed and Mr. Haslam told him about Jesus. Mr. Haslam also told him he had to be a total success in body, soul, and spirit and that having a successful family is the most important thing in life. At age thirty, with two kids, Grandpa finally learned about the love of Christ. Mr. Haslam also helped him learn how to read and write.

Because Grandpa had no education, his only hope of becoming successful was to become his own boss and create a business. In his life he had more than fourteen successful businesses and one thousand employees. He was on college boards because they needed his business sense and common sense. He helped start Christian TV in Largo and created a few well-known businesses in the Tampa Bay area. Grandpa basically made himself into something honorable when nobody said he could do it. When I asked him about the proudest thing he accomplished, he said it was leading his family to Jesus and raising his two boys. Grandpa's most important words about business are to learn to say "No, thank you," and to have consistency. Let your "yes" be yes and your "no" be no.

Grandpa has always been my role model and he is also my hero. He is an inspiration in every aspect of my life and has taught me countless things about love, wealth, and family. He always did his best to help me have the best future I can. My favorite quote of all time happens to be his own. He came up with this quote when writing his book, and I made it my senior quote this past year: "If you are not drawing your own lines you are coloring in someone else's dreams."

This quote describes Grandpa perfectly because he always taught me to think accurately for myself and to control where I go in my life. From the days singing in his truck on the way to school to our last conversation in my driveway before I went to graduate high school, Grandpa always put a smile on my face and I never enjoyed being with anyone as much as him. I will take the things he taught me and put them to use throughout my life, as should all of you. As he used to always sing, "This is the day that the Lord has made. I will rejoice and be glad in it."

Tribute from Casey Arrington:

Let me take a moment to tell you about the greatest man I have ever known, the man I was blessed enough with to be able to call my grandpa. His name is Jack Arnold Arrington. I made him a grandfather, but the greatness was already there. From the moment I was born, he has been by my side, always striving to make my life better, to raise me to be one of the finest young men alive and to instill morals and ethics that will last generations. He became my best friend, my mentor, my teacher, and my number-one role model for how to live life. There is no order of words in any language that could ever truly and fully explain the greatness the Holy Spirit instilled upon this man. Nonetheless, knowing I can never find the words to describe this incredible man won't stop me from trying.

Inside, I am falling apart looking for the words I need. If I had to choose one person who has had the biggest impact on my life, I would choose my grandpa. He is one of the most successful men I have ever known in so many things. Everyone has a different view of success, most of which involves having an overwhelmingly filled bank account, but no amount of money can bring a person full success and my grandpa understood that. In fact, he taught me that.

He managed to own many businesses, and an absolutely incredible number of employees worked for him over the years. Yet that would never stop him from waking up before me to make me breakfast, whether I wanted it or not, and he would always offer me more. If I was ever busy, he would try to help me to the fullest extent of his abilities, constantly offering to assist me in any way possible and always asking me what he could do to make things easier on me. No matter how successful he became, he always put others first one hundred percent of the time, always caring, always having a heart of servitude and strength of a leader, and what a great leader he was.

He could have let me be, let my parents teach me everything they wanted me to know, and let me figure out things on my own; but I was more blessed than that. That wasn't at all who God gave me. I had a grandfather who truly cared, who desired to see me succeed in life. No matter what, whenever he saw me, he would have something to teach me, something to give me, a lesson to be learned and wisdom to provide.

Some of my first memories of him are when I used to lie in bed as a helpless young kid, unaware of the dark world we live in, trusting Grandpa, who would always pray over me. I often wouldn't understand things he said when he would pray, but I knew he had my best interests at heart. Looking back now, I understand those things I didn't back then. Over the past few years, and even more so the past few months, he had taken to calling me much more often just to talk. If I didn't answer, he would always leave a voicemail, all of which would end with him saying, "I love you, Buddy." All he wanted to do was check on me, be part of my life, and just talk. He always had my back and changed my life for the best. I will always be thankful.

I don't even know where to begin when I say this man was a lover. So I can start with his life. When he was just a young teenager, he met my grandmother Kathy, another incredible person. When they met, he was far from the man I always knew him to be, but together they loved one another and grew together, as individuals, as a couple, and in their walk with the Lord God Almighty who loves and is love. And with the love of God, this man became unstoppable. He lived and has shown me right before my very eyes the deepest and truest love story I have ever known.

With the love of his life, he started a family and had two sons, both of which he loved as much as any one man can love someone. It was beyond words to explain the pain of his loss of his younger son, but then came into his other son's life a woman his son fell in love with. Before he knew it, I made him a grandpa. And as much as ever, my grandpa gave me the fullest extent of his love, the extent of which I have never fully understood. But I have still managed to know it. And just as much, I have loved him.

Another defining aspect of my grandpa was his incredible spirit, his unbreakable willpower, the go-getter attitude that helped him conquer and overcome everything and anything he wanted to, with the desires of the Lord placed within his heart. He was an unstoppable optimist and no matter how bad something may be, he was never going to let it get him down. He overcame so much that most people would have just caved in and fallen apart through. But he was no normal man; he had the ever-powerful spirit of the Lord living in him!

He always had a goal, always had an idea, and through everything, he always had a smile. He was contagious and anyone who got close to him for just a minute got infected with his happiness. With just a hello and a handshake, people could tell how great he was. Just in the flash of a smile he could heal a broken heart and give a person hope. If you were ever blessed enough to have even just five minutes to have a conversation with him, chances are that you would see things differently and be happier, with a better outlook and direction on and for life.

In addition to my grandpa's wonderful love and wonderful spirit of optimism, his lifestyle had a wonderful influence on me. Whenever I would look in his pantry for as long as I can remember, there were always healthy foods for the body. Things he would eat to have good health, food for the mind and food for the body. But it didn't stop there. He was also always doing. Yes, he watched TV; we all do. But if I wanted to do anything, he wouldn't wait for a single second to turn that TV off to spend time together. He always loved riding his bike and often asked me to go with him, and if he couldn't ride his bike, he would go on a walk.

His mind was always running in an attempt to do something different, to do something special, to figure out his next business move, and to show me how. But this was only part of his lifestyle. I always watched him closely. As my role model, I wanted to live like he was. I saw the way he treated his wife, the love he showed her and the true beauty they shared in their love story. I always saw the way he would drop everything for someone in need, or just to spend time with someone because he understood the importance of relationships and opportunity. This man was not someone who was going to miss an opportunity that he wouldn't have again.

He loved the Lord with all his heart and would read his Bible and pray with full authority and power of God behind him, blessed with the blood of Jesus Christ! And finally, I always saw him reading anything he could get his hands on. He committed himself to constant improvement, always learning, always striving to be better. I want to be like that, to follow in his footsteps, to learn from him in every way possible.

It's been said that you can tell a lot about a person on his or her deathbed, and I do believe that is true. There has been no point at which I haven't viewed my grandfather with deep and incredible admiration. Near the end, everything happened so suddenly, but even though this horrible disease took over his body, it never changed him nor touched his unbreakable spirit. His love stayed the same. The affection for his wife, my grandma, never ceased. She told me about how the night before I saw him, he was hardly awake, in more pain than I have ever experienced, knowing he was about to pass, yet he still held my grandmother in his arms, bringing her close and loving on her.

An image I will never forget is that as I was leaving the room he was in, he was hardly saying anything, not moving much at all, but as I was leaving the room, I looked up to see my grandmother leaning over to kiss him. But that wasn't all. I saw him kissing her back, more than once, and that is a love that can never be broken. Not even death can take away that love he built with her. Although everything happened so suddenly and there wasn't much time at all, I have seen more than enough.

155

When I first saw him for the first time on that bed, he took my hand, and he smiled at me and we told each other we loved each other and a few more things. Then later in the day he had become much less talkative and slipped into more sleep, but I was going out to dinner and had to say goodbye so I went to him and said, "Grandpa," and he looked at me and smiled and touched my chest quickly and said, "Grandson," with force and certainty. He asked where I was going and told me to have a good time, and I told him I would and I would be right back.

After that, he lost most of his ability to talk. By the end of the night, he was done talking. He could hardly say anything and couldn't even maintain the most basic functions at this point. It broke my heart, but it was time for me to go home for the night. Dad and I were saying "good night," and as we did, he woke up. With his wife, son, and I in the room, he looked at us all and then with instant vigor and determination, he lifted up both of his arms from underneath his sheets and raised them towards me.

I leaned in and, with sudden power and strength, he pulled me in to him and kissed my cheek and looked into my eyes. I told him I loved him, and he looked at me in such a way as to say with his eyes what he was unable to say with words. He succeeded, telling me everything he could through just a look.

The following day, he spent the majority of the time sleeping and had very little reaction and response to anyone, simply saying a virtually inaudible yes or no to most questions asked. But I asked him how he was doing, and he answered with power that he was "fantastic." Even when his body was broken and he was on as many drugs as he was, with the knowledge that death was close, he still had a positive and uplifting spirit of optimism and love right to the end.

Just as words can't begin to describe the incredible man my grandpa was, words will again fail me when it comes to say how much I will and do miss him. But I will and do take comfort in the knowledge that he is in a much better place now, a place that we can't even imagine the beauty of. God has finally called home his incredible servant and has a place prepared for him in Heaven. Tears will and have been shed, but in the end we can continue mourning our loss, or we can live our lives and honor him by living the lives he would have wanted us to live.

Although it sucks, and it is the worst heartbreak I have ever known, I intend to live my life in honor of him, to live this life he has helped guide to the fullest extent of my capabilities. I will never be able to thank him for what he has done for me, but I know he would desire to see me succeed even more so than he has, so I will. Someday, I will see him again. But until that day comes, I must say goodbye for now, to my dear friend and mentor.

I love you, Grandpa.

Jack A. Arrington

(October 27, 1943 - July 8, 2015)

Mr. Jack A. Arrington, 71, was called home to Glory on Wednesday, July 8th, 2015, one week after being diagnosed with pancreatic cancer. Jack passed peacefully at Haven Hospice in Chiefland with his wife Kathy and son Tim at his side.

Jack was born in Ashland, Kentucky, on October 27, 1943, to Arnold and Geneva Arrington, who have preceded him in death. Jack moved to St. Petersburg, Florida, when he was 11 and he and his wife moved full-time to their retreat home on the Suwannee River in 2010 after spending 10 beautiful years enjoying weekends there with family and friends.

Jack married his Junior High school sweetheart, Kathy Denning, in 1964. They celebrated their 51st wedding anniversary in April. Last year, on their Golden Anniversary, they renewed their wedding vows in a joyous celebration of love and life. Together they were blessed to raise two sons, Timothy Arrington, who resides in Canton, Ga. and Kenneth Arrington, who preceded his father to heaven at the age of 20.

Jack is survived by his wife Kathy, son Timothy, daughter-in-law Christy and grandchildren Casey, Corey and Cydney Arrington, who completely captured his heart. He is also survived by his sisters, Bonnie Hunt and Darlene Howland and many well-loved nieces, nephews and cousins.

Jack was a very successful entrepreneur in St. Petersburg, Florida. He and his wife started and ran over 14 businesses specializing in service and real estate enterprises. He founded Arrington Grounds Maintenance, a company that is still operating, over 40 years ago. At the time of his passing, Jack was just completing his first book, Without A Dime. The book is a humorous true-life account of his life, his love, and his business principles. He was dedicated to helping other businessman become successful in every area of their lives. As a personal business mentor and coach, he took great joy in helping others become the best they could be. On his last night at home, his wife promised that she would get that book across the finish line for him. With God being her helper, his legacy will live on to help others.

Jack and his wife accepted the Lord together in each other's arms in 1974. Jack has joyously lived out his faith daily since then. He was a member of Greenhouse Church and served on the Boards of Florida Beacon College, St. Petersburg Christian School and Suncoast Cathedral. He was also a committed supporter of New Life Solutions.

Photographs

Jack in Jr. High School

Bad Boy Jerry in Jr. High School

The hard work and saving paid off.
I bought my new Cushman Eagle

Jack in 1959 when he met Kathy at Disston Jr, High School

My winning N Stock racing car, the 1949 Oldsmobile

Don Garlits Swamp Rat that badly beat my Oldsmobile!

My 1957 Corvette. Saving all of that tip money paid off!

This 1959 Corvette was a beauty and the reward of hard work.

Kathy and I were finally married in 1964!
Our story was just beginning.

Our little family when Timmy and Kenny were young.

This is the last photo of our family together, taken at our 25th
Wedding Anniversary.

The Arrington men: Tim, Jack's father, Arnold, Ken and Jack

We celebrated our 25th Wedding Anniversary by renewing our vows before family and friends, followed by a 3 week Anniversary trip.

To celebrate our 50th Wedding Anniversary, we renewed our vows again. We were so blessed to reach this milestone.

Celebrating our 50th Wedding Anniversary with our great family.
Tim, Christy, Casey, Corey and Cydney Arrington.

Sharing a moment of joy! Every moment spent with your Love is a
treasure.

Success Secrets Legend

For Entrepreneurs Starting a Service Business

Success Secret No. 1:

Truth means agreement with reality, even if others don't get it.

Success Secret No. 2:

You first must have an understanding to have a revelation.

Success Secret No. 3:

Setting goals is one of the most important things you do to succeed in life and business.

Success Secret No. 4:

Learning from our experiences, both positive and negative, makes us more efficient and effective. We must be flexible and change our behavior or activities to improve ourselves and our situation.

Success Secret No. 5:

Personal development is the gift you give to yourself and your family. Keep learning. Always make yourself more valuable.

Success Secret No. 6:

Success means nothing without someone to share it with. No matter how much money you make, you're not living if you don't know how to find love and keep it.

Success Secret No. 7:

Opportunities are open doors to go through, but one must be ready.

Success Secret No. 8:

Remember: When the door of opportunity opens you must be ready to walk through. Don't let fear stop you.

Success Secret No. 9:

The door of opportunity should always be the right one. If it isn't, you will spend a lot of time cleaning up your own mess.

Success Secret No. 10:

Train yourself to habitually think in terms of accurate thinking. This is accomplished by considering the consequences of decisions before you make them.

Success Secret No. 11:

You have two ears and one mouth. Listen, listen, listen and learn to keep your mouth shut.

Success Secret No. 12:

Do things that you can duplicate.

Success Secret No. 13:

If you are not drawing your own lines, you are coloring in someone else's dream.

Success Secret No. 14:

We are all salespeople. We have to sell ourselves and our dreams and ideas to others in order to be successful at whatever our passion is in life.

Success Secret No. 15:

FEAR is no more than False Evidence Appearing Real. Don't give in to it!

Success Secret No. 16:

Begin with the end in mind and become an expert in your chosen area.

Success Secret No. 17:

Always keep your word or don't give it.

Success Secret No. 18:

Practice over and over in your mind in order to win or be successful. You must visualize success.

Success Secret No. 19:

The most important assets are the human kind.

Success Secret No. 20:

Watch out for time wasters. You only get one life, one finite amount of time. Spend it wisely.

Success Secret No. 21:

Look for the humor in every situation. Then figure out what you can learn from it.

Success Secret No. 22:

Never let your fear of failure keep you from trying new things.

Success Secret No. 23:

To win or be successful, practice again and again. Visualize your steps to success over and over. Then put them in motion.

Success Secret No. 24:

Don't be afraid to make the right paradigm shifts in your attitude, outlook, and company. Sometimes you need to change your business model to grow your company. Sometimes you need to change your thinking to grow yourself.

Success Secret No. 25:

Possessing the Holy Spirit in one's life allows one to be tapped into the wisdom of the God of the universe.

Success Secret No. 26:

A problem defined is half-solved.

Success Secret No. 27:

Practice preparation, perseverance, and consistency. Make the most of every day!

Recommended Books

If you change yourself for the better just one-third of one percent each day, in three hundred days you are one hundred percent smarter than you were!

I strongly suggest improving yourself and your life and business knowledge by reading (or listening to) the following classics:

1. The Bible (The instruction book for man)

2. *Without A Dime by* Jack Arrington

3. *Wild at Heart* by John Eldredge

4. *Rookie Smarts* by Liz Wiseman

5. *The Power of Positive Thinking* by Norman Vincent Peale

6. *Think and Grow Rich* by Napoleon Hill

7. *The Magic of Thinking Big* by Dave J. Schwartz, Ph.D.

8. *Rich Dad Poor Dad* by Robert T. Kiyosaki

9. *The 7 Habits of Highly Effective People* by Stephen R. Covey

10. *The Art of Exceptional Living* by Jim Rohn

11. *The Compound Effect* by Darren Hardy

12. *The One Minute Manager* by Ken Blanchard and Spencer Johnson

13. *Acres of Diamonds* by Russell H. Conwell

14. *As A Man Thinketh* by James Allen

Businesses Owned by Jack Arrington

1. Jack Arrington, Personal Business Coach/Motivational Speaker

2. Arrington Grounds Maintenance, LLC

3. Other separate businesses under the same Company name of AGM included:

   a. Buying and selling large equipment

   b. Buying and selling vehicles

   c. Buying and selling service companies

4. Arrington Properties, LLC

5. Good Guys Real Estate, LLC

6. Laughing Grass Fertilization and Insect Control, LLC

7. Precious People Real Estate Rentals, LLC

8. Pick Up Properties Real Estate, LLC

9. Wise Apps, LLC

10. Arrington Pump and Sprinkler Maintenance, LLC

11. Arrington Tree Service, LLC

12. Sun-n-Fun Pool Services, LLC

13. Arrington Landscaping and Nursery, LLC

14. Orange Blossom Lawn and Landscaping

15. Arrington Rental Properties

16. Jack A. Arrington Grounds Maintenance

17. Author of *Turf Grass is Gold*

Endnotes

1 Paradigms author and businessman Joel A. Barker,
https://www.brainyquote.com/quotes/joel_a_barker_158200

2. Motivational speaker and author Jim Rohn on his own Facebook page,
3.12.2013,
https://www.facebook.com/OfficialJimRohn/posts/10152620801285635

3. Conwell, R. H. (1968). *Acres of diamonds: Russell Conwell's inspiring classic about opportunity.* Kansas City, Mo.: Hallmark Editions.

4. "Goodnite, Sweetheart, Goodnite" by Calvin Carter and James "Pookie" Hudson was written in 1953, and recorded in 1954 by the doo-wop group The Spaniels.

5. Proverbs 23:7, The Bible, King James Version.

6. Kiyosaki, R. T., & Lechter, S. L. (1998). *Rich dad, poor dad: What the rich teach their kids about money that the poor and middle class do not!.* Paradise Valley, Ariz: TechPress.

7. Proverbs 23:7, The Bible, King James Version.

8. The Museum of Drag Racing is located at 13700 SW 16th Ave., Ocala, FL 34473.

9. Van Rooy, David (2014). *Trajectory: 7 career strategies to take you from where you are to where you want to be.* New York: AMACOM, American Management Association.

Made in the USA
Monee, IL
16 December 2019